IMAGES OF ENGLAND

CROSSLEY
HEATH SCHOOL

IMAGES OF ENGLAND

CROSSLEY HEATH SCHOOL

ROSE TAYLOR, ANDREW KAFEL
AND RUSSELL SMITH

TEMPUS

Frontispiece: Crossley Heath School, 2005.

First published 2006

Tempus Publishing Limited
The Mill, Brimscombe Port,
Stroud, Gloucestershire, GL5 2QG
www.tempus-publishing.com

British Library Cataloguing in Publication Data.
A catalogue record for this book is available from the British Library.

ISBN 0 7524 3866 2

Typesetting and origination by Tempus Publishing Limited.
Printed in Great Britain.

Contents

Acknowledgements

We acknowledge the invaluable help given by the following: The 'Friday Group' – being those who regularly met at school and worked conscientiously and tirelessly on the projects to both store and catalogue the archives, and to produce this book. We met every Friday and were sustained by coffee, cakes, biscuits and many school dinners! This loyal group led by Rose Taylor is: Vernon Brearley, Andrew Kafel, Russell Smith and Philip Webb. Others have joined in at various stages, these being notably: Gordon Normanton, John Davey, Rod Eastwood and the late Malcolm Bamforth.

Thanks also go to: John Bunch, former headmaster, whose comprehensive knowledge of both Heath School and Crossley Heath School was invaluable; The Crossley Heath Association (PTA) for their enthusiastic support; Sophie Cox, former student at Crossley Heath, for her photograph; Steve Eggleton, head of biology at Crossley Heath, for a photograph; Fotek School Portraits; *Halifax Courier*, without whose wonderful photographs we would not have been able to produce this book; Peter Hand, former teacher at Heath School and Crossley Heath School, whose research documents were comprehensive and thorough; Barbara Ingham, former pupil and boarder at Crossley and Porter School, for reminiscences; Michael Jackson, site manager at Crossley Heath, for facts (and stories!); Brian Moore, former student at Crossley and Porter School, for his photograph; Mike Newton, former head of physics at Crossley Heath, for his photographs; Northlight Studios, Elland, for their digital photography; The Scottish Football Museum for use of the photograph of Andrew Watson; Pat Sewell, principal archivist at West Yorkshire Archive Service; J.R. Stafford, former teacher at Crossley and Porter School, for his photographs; and Geoffrey Washington, a Heath old boy, for a photograph; Philip Webb for help with captions.

Introduction

The Crossley Heath School is steeped in 420 years of tradition and has survived many different phases in its long history to become a central part of the community of Halifax and a hugely successful school.

1985 saw probably the biggest change when Crossley and Porter amalgamated with Heath to form the Crossley Heath School. Two schools came together, each with a history attached to it, and the idea for this book originated from a group of people interested in preserving the stories of the past for future generations.

Members of both the Heath Old Boys' Association and the Crossley and Porter Old Scholars' Association realised that the knowledge they had and the memories they thought were important might be lost unless they were recorded. This group of people are the 'Friday Group', detailed in the acknowledgements section of this book.

Also, when former headmaster John Bunch retired in 2001, he bequeathed an abundance of archive material to the safekeeping of the school Learning Resource Centre, adding to what was already a vast and growing collection there. With an increasing number of enquiries about former pupils and staff via the Internet, boosted by mounting public interest in genealogy, a random collection of boxes and bags did not do justice to the huge quantity of valuable information.

A process began, to organise, categorise, catalogue and store everything – a task one might assume to be at the heart of librarianship. However, this collection ranged from meat platters from the orphanage to large charters with wax seals. In respect of the history of Heath Grammar School, whilst there is little readily in print, there is a substantial body of work providing a significant amount of detail available to the dedicated researcher. It was therefore difficult to choose what to exclude in this largely photographic record. There are hundreds of documents and letters and other material, but of greatest interest to most people are the photographs. These remain the focus of our book – the thing that brings the history alive. The school is lucky to own such a collection, mostly preserved in very good condition, from Victorian times to date. Our research has unearthed a multitude of facts, yet has posed for us new and often unanswered questions. This book represents the best of what we have and doesn't profess to be a comprehensive history.

All of our photographs have been digitally recorded and, in fact, many school events of today are recorded and stored only in this way. Modern technology allows the faces of those students, who have passed through Heath and Crossley and Porter over more than a hundred years, to be seen on a computer screen as though they were at school today and not frozen in time on a page.

The seventeenth-century statue of Dr John Favour, vicar of Halifax 1593-1623 and founder of Heath Grammar School. It was restored in 1993 after an appeal by the Old Boys which coincided with the 400th anniversary of Dr Favour's arrival in Halifax. The bust stands in Halifax Parish Church, where Founder's Day used to be celebrated annually in June.

one

The Beginning
1585-1879

The first significant date in the history of Heath Grammar School is 15 February 1585, when Queen Elizabeth signed the charter establishing 'the free grammar school of Queen Elizabeth'. Dr John Favour, vicar of Halifax from 1593 to 1624, is regarded as the founder of the school, being responsible for obtaining the piece of land upon which the first school was built – two acres of barren heath land donated by Henry Farrar in 1597. This, together with money donated by Sir John Savile, enabled the first Heath School to be built, opening in 1600. Heath Grammar School was built by the Ackroyds of Hipperholme, whose fame derived from their university buildings in Oxford, including the Bodleian Library. The two-storeyed building of about fifty feet by twenty feet cost £120. The Ackroyds received their contract price plus £20 for building it so well, and another £20 for building it 'expeditiously'. There was a schoolhouse, and a house for the master adjacent to it. The old road leading to it became Free School Lane. Between 1600 and 1635 the governors of Heath raised enough money to buy some land, including Hutt Farm in Ovenden and Northfieldgate Farm in Northowram.

In 1600 Richard Wilkinson was master, followed in 1603 by Robert Byrron, who served until 1620. School furniture was bought and the first charter said, 'the bringing up, teaching and instructing of Children and Youth of the said Parish and Vicarage of Halifax, and also of other Villages and Hamlets near adjoining unto the same ... in Grammar, and other good Learning, to be continued for ever'.

Two sections of the original school remain today – a stone plaque and the apple and pear window. The window, which is unglazed, was constructed by John Ackroyd (1556-1613) & Sons, masons, and formed part of the gable wall of the original building. Believed to be special to this region, construction of these round windows depended on the use of templates, probably made of wood, which could be reused if desired to make more windows of identical

design and dimensions. It was moved intact to its present site in 1879. At the front of the 1879 school, set above the front door, is a replica window, this one glazed and with an inscription 'GRAMMER' – the word quite wrongly spelt.

In 1603 Dr Favour 'bestowed on the School a fair Couper's Dictionary, and a fair Greek Lexicon, and a fair English Bible'. These dictionaries, dated 1598, were recorded in 1879 as in good condition apart from the title pages. Of particular interest is the graffiti, with some signatures dating back over the centuries. The books are housed in the current school library and, to put them into context, substantially pre-date Samuel Johnson's dictionary of 1755. His was, of course, considered to be the first great English dictionary whilst those presented by Dr Favour were Latin and Greek.

It is documented that in 1612 school began at 6 a.m. and finished at 5 p.m., with a break from 11 a.m. to 1 p.m. Sunday was free, as was Thursday afternoon, and Saturday morning was given over to religious instruction. A master was in charge, assisted by an usher (a sort of deputy), who was often unqualified. The boys were expected to make their way to school without noise or playing and to take off their caps to those they met. Whilst in school they spoke only in Latin, not English.

Elephas, Elephantis, elephantus

An Oliphant, the greatest of al foure footed beastes, having his fore legges longer than his hinder, and five toes on his feete undivided: his snoute or nose so long and in such forme as it serveth him in neede of a hande to all uses. He hath iiii teeth on either side to grinde his meate, and with all two mightie tuskes bowing downeward wherewith he fighteth. Of all beasts he is most gentle, tractable, wittie to understand or be taught any kinde of thing. He never toucheth againe the female, that he hath seasoned: winter or cold he may hardly abide. It is written that if he meete a man in wildernesse out of any way, gentlely he will go before him, and leade him into the way againe. In battle he will carie a man wounded back into the middle of the armie, that he may be defended and relieved. He liveth 200 yeares, or at least 120 yeares.

Above left: Elephas, Elephantis, elephantus, excerpt from Latin dictionary, 1598.

An Oliphant, the greatest of al foure footed beastes, having his fore legges longer than his hinder, and five toes on his feete undivided: his snoute or nose so long and in such forme as it serveth him in neede of a hande to all uses. He hath iiii teeth on either side to grinde his meate, and with all two mightie tuskes bowing downeward wherewith he fighteth. Of all beasts he is most gentle, tractable, wittie to understand or be taught any kinde of thing. He never toucheth againe the female, that he hath seasoned: winter or cold he may hardly abide. It is written that if he meete a man in wildernesse out of any way, gentlely he will go before him, and leade him into the way againe. In battle he will carie a man wounded back into the middle of the armie, that he may be defended and relieved. He liveth 200 yeares, or at least 120 yeares.

Charter of Confirmation obtained from King George II in 1729. The original charter of Elizabeth I cannot be traced.

There were school governors as laid down in the original charter, but a century later it disappeared and the school was in some disarray from neglect and poor control. It is probable that many of the rents had not been collected for several years. An opportunity was taken, upon the death of Thomas Lister, the master from 1688-1728, to recreate and confirm the charter, and in 1729 this was signed by Queen Caroline, in the absence abroad of George II. Incredibly, this too is in school complete with its seal.

None of the processes happened without a great deal of correspondence and business, led largely by Mr Richard Sterne, uncle of eighteenth-century writer Laurence Sterne of Wood Hall. A new set of governors requested a set of statutes to clarify the duties and obligations of governors, masters and pupils. There was a succession of masters throughout the eighteenth century, bringing mixed fortunes, but with the leadership of Richard Hudson (1771-1782) and Gough Willis Kempson (1783-1788), Heath entered a period where it flourished. The curriculum was broadened from just Latin, Greek and English and the school and schoolhouse were enlarged. Whilst still only a one-room building, the school could take sixty boys, and the schoolhouse was big enough for the master, his family and boarders. In 1773 the master's salary was £50 per annum and the usher's £30.

The flourishing of the school must in some part have reflected the expanding commercial activity of Halifax, leading to an increased demand for education. Also, the end of the eighteenth century saw some changes in land ownership and use, returning a profit to the school. By 1812, the first bank account was opened and Heath was led by Robert Wilkinson (1789-1839), succeeded by John Henry Gooch, then Thomas Cox. By 1826 there were several boarders and thirty-five free scholars; in 1854 they totalled more than seventy, declining to

The drawing in 1879 by W.H. Stopford shows the interior of the 1597 Heath School building. The benches, which were called forms, were used by all age groups of students, and the modern Heath Grammar School continued using this term until its closure in 1985, hence the reference to newcomers to the school being known as 'first formers'. The apple and pear window still exists, as does the heraldic shield (top right) which was dedicated to the Waterhouse family who were school benefactors. Both are in the current Heath building.

only twenty-seven in 1859. This period saw both Gooch and Cox thwarted in their attempts to make Heath a public school, as was the case with similar endowed schools. Changes, in every respect, affected the fortunes of Heath, including competition from other local schools, missed opportunities to change and broaden the curriculum, accusations by local people of governors misusing charity funds, easier use of transport (including the new railways) allowing pupils to travel elsewhere, and inadequacy of income from rent to keep up with the pace of change – all at a time of general economic decline. Plans to sell land to generate income were postponed until the 1860s.

In 1869, the Endowed Schools Act sought to reorganise education, with Heath fighting (but failing) to avoid this by claiming to be a Church of England School, and having reorganisation imposed upon it in 1873. This involved appointing local councillors to the governing body and a widening of the curriculum to meet changing times. Gooch had added mathematics to the curriculum, and Cox added 'a systematic study of English Literature and the French Language, and a more extensive acquaintance with Divinity'. There was also provision for drawing, drill, science, chemistry, geography, history, art and book-keeping.

Left: A lithograph of John Henry Gooch, headmaster 1840-1861, by Edwin Cocking, 1856. Gooch succeeded Robert Wilkinson, who had been head for fifty years (1789-1839). Over time, Heath had ceased taking boarders and consequently had failed to attract students from further afield who wanted a classical education. Gooch had been a scholar of Trinity College, Cambridge and rebuilt academic success, with scholars progressing to university. He introduced all branches of mathematics to the school syllabus.

Below: The Foundation Stone plaque, dated 1598, was transferred to the headmaster's house, built in 1830. After becoming a sixth form annexe the house was sold in 1991 and is now a doctor's surgery. The inscription in Latin translates as 'The land was bad and barren, but through the Grace of Queen Elizabeth, the school was erected and it was hoped it would be a blessing to the people'.

1809 Dec 20 Heath School, near Halifax.
              Mas Grimshaw

		L	S	D
Teaching and Writing *half a year*		3	13	6
Board		17	6	6
		21	0	0

Money laid out in the School.

		L	S	D
French Master	Play Ground 1/6	0	1	6
Dancing Master	Seat in the Church 2/6	0	2	6
Drawing Master	Fire and Candles 5/3	0	5	3
Paper, Quills, Copy Books, and Pencils 12/0½ newspaper		0	13	0½
Ink 1/6 Books 5/6		0	17	0
Money laid out in the Family.	Hair cut 1/6	0	1	6
The Use of Sheets and Towels 5/3	Letters 9/8	0	14	11
Shoestrings and Garters 1/	Allowance Money 4/-	0	5	0
Washing 16/	extra ditto 6/6	1	2	6
Apothecary Watchmaker Glover				
Draper and Taylor 3/8	Shoes cleaned 3/6	0	7	2
Shoemaker 11/10 Hosier Salt of Lemon 1/		0	12	10
Servants 10/6 Linen repaired 4 night caps 8/6		0	19	4
Candles for the Family 3/6 ... 15/9		0	19	3
Hatter Windows mended 1/		0	1	0
		7	2	9½
		21	0	0
		28 2	9½	

One of the many original documents held now at Crossley Heath School, this details, for master Grimshaw, a half year's account for education and board from 1809. Cox's *History of Heath* contains a partial school list created from names scribbled in the old school dictionaries (mentioned in the introduction to this chapter), although Grimshaw is not on that list. Interestingly, he would appear to have broken a window, for which he was charged a shilling.

1600-1603	Richard Wilkinson
1603-1629	Robert Byrron
1629-164?	Francis Cockman
1650 (mentioned)	March or Marsh
1651-1666	Paul Greenwood
1666-1688	John Doughty
1688-1728	Thomas Lister
1730-1731	Christopher Jackson
1731-1733	Edward Topham
1733-1744	John Holdsworth
1744-1753	Samuel Ogden
1753-1771	Thomas West
1771-1782	Richard Hudson
1783-1788	Gough Willis Kempson
1789-1839	Robert Wilkinson
1840-1861	John Henry Gooch
1861-1883	Thomas Cox
1887-1908	Archibald William Reith
1908-1916	William Edwards
1916-1935	Owen Richard Augustus Byrde
1935-1946	Douglas Joseph David Smith
1946-1971	Walter Ronald Swale
1971-1984	Albert Crosby
1984-1985	John Trevor Bunch

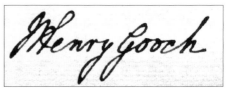

Above left: Headmasters of Heath Grammar School.

Left: Albert Crosby, who was head 1971-1984, followed W.R. Swale as headmaster and led Heath School through difficult times when the local authority wished to close the school and introduce a comprehensive system of education.

Above left: Thomas Cox, a scholar of St John's College, Cambridge, was the final headmaster at the old Heath building, from 1861-1883. Seen here mortar board in hand, he broadened the curriculum to include English literature and French language. He wrote *A Popular History of the Grammar School of Queen Elizabeth at Heath* – a book long out of print.

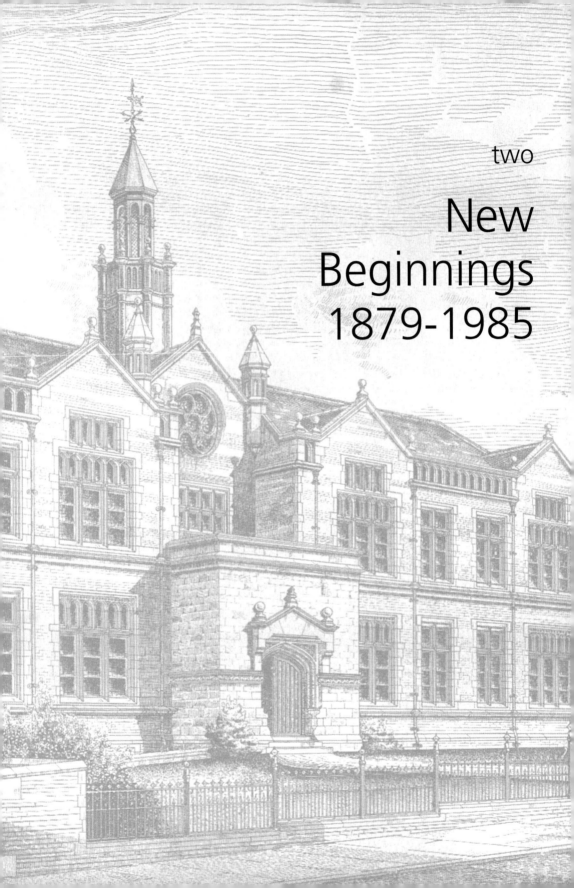

two

New
Beginnings
1879-1985

The governors decided that to accomplish planned changes to Heath they would entirely rebuild the school, with the sale of land in Skircoat providing funds. The ambitious project eventually cost £10,000 and architects Leeming & Leeming designed the new school. The new building, opened in 1879, housed sixteen classrooms, art and science rooms, a library and a gym. It could accommodate 250 boys, but none boarding, although the new master's house did have room for five boarders.

Despite all of this, with the departure of Thomas Cox in 1883, Heath School closed until 1887, being reported in the media as 'hopelessly insolvent'. Certainly, there were many rival schools providing competition for Heath, as could be seen in advertising in the *Halifax Courier*. No official or public explanation states why in 1883 Heath School had only one master and thirteen boys, but happily, with Halifax citizens taking on the role of guarantors and with the appointment in 1887 of A.W. Reith, the school reopened and he stayed for twenty-one years. In 1897 Hutt Farm and Northfieldgate Farm were sold. That year too saw financially successful tercentenary celebrations and Heath saw a gradual and sustained gain in academic success and popularity.

Staff of Heath School in 1879, the year the new school building opened. Headmaster the Revd Thomas Cox is third from the left. Others are junior master Mr J. Clayton, mathematical master Mr W. Sadd, French teacher Monsieur Poire, drawing teacher Mr W. Stopford, and drill teacher Mr T. Morley. Boys were admitted from the age of eight, transferring to the senior department at fourteen and staying until nineteen. Entrance exams to Heath covered reading, writing and arithmetic.

Having operated as an independent school up until 1922, Heath was then faced with a choice of staying with a government grant or opting for a county council one. They chose the latter and in 1926 Heath became a state grammar school maintained by Halifax Borough Council. Following Reith, Heath was led by the headships, successively, of William Edwards and O.R.A. Byrde, until 1935.

Between 1916 and 1935, electric lights replaced gas and the school grounds were further developed with the addition of tennis courts, and in 1922 the Kensington sports field was bought.

Records show that besides academic success, Heath was notable for its concerts, drama, music, camping, Scouts and sport, producing several notable characters over the years.

The *Heathen*, the school magazine, appeared in 1918 and many copies survive in the Crossley Heath School library. The junior school is occasionally and fleetingly mentioned in the *Heathen* and certainly in the 1920s there were three forms.

As elsewhere, the Second World War impacted on the school, with staff and older pupils going into the armed forces. Heath memorial gates, erected in 1949, commemorate those who did not return.

The final series of headmasters until the closure of Heath saw D.J.D. Smith carry the school through the period of the 1944 Education Act. Parents were relieved of the payment of fees and the junior school had to close, with remaining boys transferring to Crossley and Porter School – the first Crossley Heathens! 1946 saw the arrival of head W.R. Swale, who had to adapt to the pace of change in post-war Britain whilst defending the grammar school tradition and its academic ethos. Albert Crosby took the school through the period from 1971, when frequent government plans might have seen Heath merge with other schools as part of comprehensive education plans. Under the final headship of J.T. Bunch in 1984, a decision was taken by the Secretary of State for Education that Heath would close in August 1985, just six months after celebrating 400 years in existence. The popularity of those celebrations was tangible evidence of the esteem in which the school was held.

Football team from 1891/2. Five boys can be seen wearing caps, presumably for their sporting excellence; the system of awarding colours continued into the 1960s. From left to right, back row (standing): Sergeant Dillon, ? Dodgson, S. Storey, E. Child, D. Culpan, S. Chambers, T. Davis, J.P. Martin Dupre. Middle row (kneeling): D. Waite, B. Longbottom. Front row (sitting): ? Whiteley, A. Cunliffe, J.H. Walton (behind), E. Sookes (?) (captain), S. Rhodes, S.J. Flossman, P. Crabtree.

Football team from 1903/4 taken at the front of the headmaster's house. Notice the shirts embroidered with HGS, the leather 'button ball' and boots with early leather studs. Football continued to be played at Heath until 1928. From left to right, back row (standing): W.E. Jennings, S. Balme, C. Reynolds, C.D. Ellis, A. Lewin, S.J.E. Sargeant, J.P. Martin, S. Topham. Seated: J.S. Winter, S. Teal, T.W. Berry, F.W. Milling (captain), E.J. Sutcliffe.

Fives team from 1909. This was possibly the very first fives team to play the game at Heath although the whereabouts of the courts at that time are open to conjecture. J.H. Whitley, MP for Halifax and who went on to become Speaker of the House of Commons, presented the known courts to Heath School in 1924. The first four, from left to right: H. Whitley, R.E. Dalzell, F. Clegg, E.B. Petty.

Right: William Edwards, headmaster 1908-1916. Several masters left the school to serve in the armed forces but Edwards led Heath to first place in the Oxford Local examination results in 1915. Having moved to Heath from Bradford Grammar School, he returned there as head in 1916.

Above right: Archibald William Reith (headmaster 1887-1908), who led Heath Grammar School after its reopening. He died in 1908 and was commemorated by a plaque in Halifax Parish Church. The praiseworthy epitaph on this ends: 'and by his untiring labours and unwavering fidelity administered it (the school) with such devotion that, when at length having fulfilled his task he was snatched away by death in the Year of Our Saviour 1908, he left it to his successors pre-eminent for the number of its pupils, for the greatness of its distinction, and above all for the courtesy of its manners'.

Pictured in his study is O.R.A. Byrde (Oscar), one of the renowned headmasters of Heath Grammar School. His headship lasted from 1916 until his retirement in1935, during which time the school gathered great academic strength, achieving results surpassed by few equivalent schools at the time. A verse by a boy at the time summarised him thus: 'Old Oscar was a kindly man, the school he simply loved it. He never had to open a door because his tummy shoved it!'. Colleagues paid tribute to a generous, warm-hearted, sympathetic and loyal friend when he died in 1936.

Teachers at the annual Heath School camp, Primrose Valley, Filey, around 1934-35. The boys learnt lessons 'of loyalty and cooperation for the common good', although they would have also recalled fishing, walking and playing football. The water was found to be too cold for bathing by the majority! Mr Byrde, the headmaster, attended on the Sunday for prayers, bringing with him more food! From left to right, back row: Ben Young, -?-, Cecil Mackley, Eric 'Biddy' Taylor, -?-. Seated: Arthur 'Tough' Owen, Frank 'Whisky' Haigh.

Heath Junior School cricket team 1930/31, in cricket attire in need of whitening judging by their appearance! This season they played five games; they had two wins, two losses and a tie. From left to right, back row: K.P. Thomas, S.J. Hollway, G.J. Normanton, G.D. Greenwood, B. Matthews, R.T. Stephen. Middle row: R. Dobson, H. Robertson (captain), D.A. Ingram. Front row: J.P. Feather, J.D. Eccles, P.L. Shaw.

Rugby First XV, 1935/6. As usual, Heath Grammar School played Crossley and Porter during their season, and in 1936 were keen to avenge their previous 11-5 defeat. At five minutes before time with the score at 6-9, Heath managed a last-minute victory, by making the score 11-9. From left to right, back row: K. Ramsden, D. Gledhill, R. Mitchell, A. Haller, K. Riley, A. Guest, E. Clarry, G. Burgoyne. Front row: G. Dalzell, H. Wilson, J. Riley, Mr A. Bilbrough, H. Pitchforth, R. Bedford, J. Lewin, H. Sheard.

Heath School performance of *Coriolanus*, 1935, with several teachers taking lead parts including Mr Bilbrough as Coriolanus and Mr Mackley as Menenius. Older boys playing Roman aristocrats, contrasting with youngsters playing the mob attired in soiled and rather brief costumes, provided a 'never-failing' source of amusement to observers, according to the review in the *Heathen*.

Heath School Camp at St Helen's, Isle of Wight, 16–30 August 1938. In 1939 the camp was at Bridgwater and a circular was sent to parents in which the onset of the Second World War was clearly expected. However, if war were to be declared, 'every effort will be made to return boys safely to their homes'. The camps were strictly ordered with duty rosters, the earliest of which, at 6 a.m., ensured that boys stoked the fires, fetched the milk and stirred the porridge – minor duties compared to others who had to peel potatoes or inspect latrines!

Right: D.J.D. Smith, MA, was headmaster of Heath School from 1935-1946. He was a senior scholar of Trinity College, Cambridge and led the school to great academic success. The *Heathen* saw him as the lubricating oil that kept the school machine running smoothly in spite of the staffing difficulties engendered by the Second World War. He was highly regarded, combining the classical tradition of Heath with modern educational methods introduced by the 1944 Education Act. At this time, Paul Barker, future headmaster of Crossley and Porter School and first head of Crossley Heath School, was a pupil.

Below: The memorial gates to Heath School, made by Wilfred Dowson of Kirk Forge, Kirkbymoorside, were unveiled in 1949 to honour the forty old boys who fell in the Second World War. The Latin inscription *Digni et vos este favore* translates as 'Be you also worthy of Favour', the 'Favour' being Dr Favour, founder of Heath School in 1597. The Latin inscription was written by Arthur Owen, the senior classics master, and was submitted to politician Enoch Powell, acknowledged to be a leading expert in Latin, for his approval. He is reported to have described it as 'brilliant'.

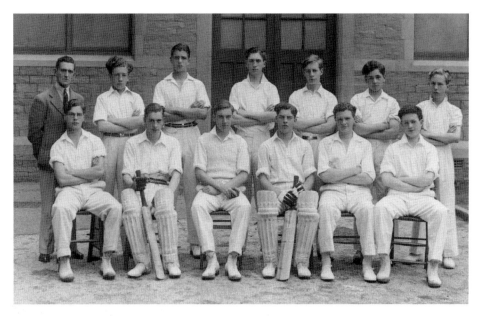

Cricket continued to be played throughout the war years and Mr C.H. Place ('Chuss') served as sportsmaster, firstly at Crossley and Porter and then at Heath, and remained at the school until Harry Birchall returned from army service to resume his post. The year 1942 was a successful season against Crossley and Porter, with Heath's first and second teams winning. Pictured is the First XI; from left to right, back row: Mr C.H. Place, G. Scholfield, A. Naylor, T. Stansfield, W. Tordoff, H. Birch, G. Sutcliffe. Seated: R. Lumb, H. Shackleton, T. Atkins, J. Shoesmith, P. Sutcliffe, J. Clarke.

Heath prefects 1946/47, the year in which W.R. Swale became headmaster, having served in the army as lieutenant-colonel. Swale considered his prefects to be 'Pillars of the Establishment'. From left to right, back row: -?-, Joe Walmsley, Gus Harris, Malcolm McDonald, -?-, -?-. Front row: -?-, -?-, J.B. Capindale, W.R. Swale (headmaster), K. Seward-Shaw, Ian Manson, D. Jackson.

This informal photograph of the school choir was taken on Speech Day 1949, on the steps from the hall leading down to the lower playground. As a group of enthusiastic amateurs, and at a time when less emphasis was placed on music in school, the school choir and orchestra were extremely successful. Included are several teachers. From left to right, back row: 6th, Eric Taylor, 7th, Arthur Holt, 8th, Norman Gain, 9th, Harry Lee, 11th, Frank Haigh.

Heath Grammar School Orchestra and Choir 1950/51. This ensemble is being conducted by the late Dudley Holroyd, a talented musical student who became choirmaster and organist at Bath Abbey from 1967-1985. The orchestra is clearly supplemented by invited musicians but the choir sang every morning in assembly, which always consisted of prayers, a reading, school news and a hymn.

Sheridan's popular eighteenth-century comedy of manners, *The Rivals*, produced by Heath Grammar School Dramatic Society, 1949/50. Barrie Ingham, seen standing in the middle, attended Heath from 1942-1950 and became a leading light in the dramatic society. Having completed service in the Royal Artillery after school, he spent time at the Manchester Library Theatre Company and subsequently worked with many stage companies, including London's Old Vic Theatre, the Royal Shakespeare and the Mermaid. He played in hit musicals in New York and appeared in over 200 television and motion pictures.

The Ilkley RUFC Sevens Tournament was extremely popular amongst Yorkshire grammar schools. This team achieved a resounding victory for Heath School in their first year of entry, the first of a hat-trick of victories in 1951-53. J.P. Horrocks-Taylor went on to play for Heath Old Boys' RUFC, Halifax RUFC, Cambridge University, Leicester, Middlesbrough, England and the British Lions. From left to right, back row: F.W. Normington, J.N. Dixon, T.D. Gamson, J.G. Farrar. Front row: K.E. Humphreys, M. Bamforth (captain), J.P. Horrocks-Taylor.

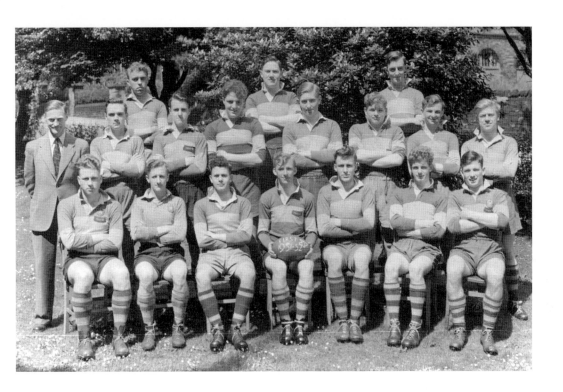

Above: 1951/52 was a good season for this rugby First XV, winning thirteen games, losing only three and drawing against Heath Old Boys. Sportsmaster Harry Birchall, injured during wartime army service, had returned to run very successful sports teams and helped Heath win a huge reputation. From left to right, back row: J. Hoggard, E. Donnelly, K. Ackroyd. Middle row: F. Normington, C. Bowes, J. Esmond, J. Stoddart, R. Smith, K. Johnson, A. Greenwood. Front row: T. Gamson, J.G. Farrar, D. Horrocks-Taylor, K. Humphreys, J.P. Horrocks-Taylor, J. Dixon, D. Gillett.

Right: Fives team, 1952, on the front lawn of Heath Grammar School. During the season the team travelled as far as Durham and Sheffield, although Crossley and Porter also had a fives court and during 1952 Heath played against them twice. The first match was disastrous but later in the season, after fitness training, Heath beat them 11-1. The fives courts remain in use to this day. Standing from left to right: J.G. Farrar, J.P. Horrocks-Taylor, M. Taylor. Seated: P. Kiddle. The latter was later awarded an OBE for services to sound technology.

Cricket First XI, 1952 – a particularly successful season including F. Normington taking six wickets for nineteen against Rishworth. This was Mr Atkins' last season before leaving to take up a post at Bingley Grammar School. From left to right, back row: Mr S. Atkins, P. Haley, A. Jagger, T. Gamson, K. Hartley, A. Greenwood, D. Verity, A. Stott. Sitting: G. Lawrence, M. Horrocks-Taylor, J.P. Horrocks-Taylor, J.G. Farrar, J. Esmond, F. Normington, J. Mitchell.

Athletics team, 1953. This was a successful year for Heath, winning all four shields at the Halifax and District Grammar Schools' Sports Association – junior, intermediate, senior and the overall championship. From left to right, back row: K. Johnson, A. Parry, A. Robinson, T. Gamson, J. Esmond, P. Clayton, M. Beaufort-Jones, G. Harrison, Mr Harry Birchall. Middle: F. Normington, R. Watling, A. Greenwood, C. Ambler, D. Skirrow, G. Carr, P. Benson, R. Greenwood, B. Seal, A. Coward. Front row: C. Wood, C. Dormer, S. Watkin, A. Jagger, S. Milner, C. Weston, J. Payne.

The 1960/61 cross-country team easily won the inter-grammar school competition (with seven schools competing), taking the senior championship shield. From left to right, back row: M. Hinchcliffe, G. Gledhill, Mr J.M. Blythe, R. Fox, T. Binns. Front row: G. Hesselden, J. Kenyon, A. Tatham, B. Marney, A. Shannon. Malcolm Blythe continued his teaching career at Crossley Heath after amalgamation, becoming head of chemistry.

The rugby sevens team, winners again of the Ilkley schools' knock-out competition in 1962. This victorious team beat Queen Elizabeth's Grammar School 13-5 in the final, a match which was, according to the *Heathen*, 'not exciting, as Heath always had the situation well in hand!'. From left to right, back row: D. Backhouse, D. Brittain, H. Blakeborough, J. Helliwell, Mr Harry Birchall. Front row: J. Broughton, A. Wilkinson, I. Booth, C. Holmes, R. Broughton. The latter won a blue for Oxford University and played for Yorkshire, as did Booth. Both played for Halifax RUFC.

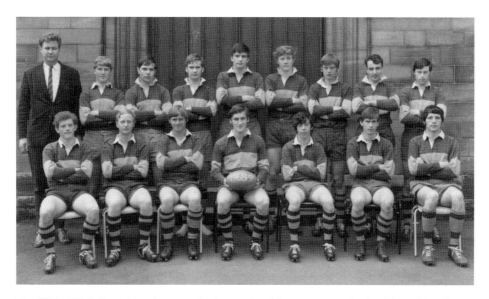

First XV of 1968/9, perhaps the most pleasing result of the season was the thrashing of Crossley and Porter 32-5, who, however, gained revenge by beating Heath 6-5 in a mudbath at Broomfield in the last match of the season. From left to right, back row: Mr R. Bellerby, P. Smith, P. Sutcliffe, C. Maude, S. Lum, K. Gaynor, J. Bradley, K. Binns, M. Firth. Front row: R. Smithies, C. Bradley, R. Jackson, R. Brearley, K. Davis, R. Sutcliffe, R. Noble.

Heath Grammar School staff, June 1971. W.R. Swale was headmaster from 1946-1971 and, together with the front row in particular, represented hundreds of years of teaching at Heath and provided the bedrock stability required. Jack White and Andrew Connell are old boys of the school. From left to right, back row: D. Morton, R. Bardelang, A. Hardill, P. Smith. Middle row: P. Hand, S. Squires, J. White, D. Southcombe, J. Pickersgill, A. Barnett, A. Connell, A. Guy, J. Mackie, J. Hampshire, J. Blythe. Front row: H. Birchall, H. Lee, D. Hallowes, A. Owen, W. Swale, H. Morris, F. Haigh, G. Littlefair, Mrs C. Livermore.

As head of music, J. Michael Hampshire (extreme left) built an outstanding choir in the 1970s which performed at several venues in England and abroad. They are shown here, complete with gowns, outside Bath Abbey on a nine-day visit in 1974. Bath Abbey choirmaster was Dudley Holroyd, a Heath old boy. While the abbey choir was away, the school choir took over their musical operation for a week. They performed as a 'cathedral voluntary choir', including singing evensong almost every day and putting on a finale concert on Saturday 10 August.

The Devil's Disciple, by G.B. Shaw and produced by J.T. Bunch with Heath Dramatic Society in March 1973, was a taste of things to come since the poster proudly boasted that after years of single-sex productions, this one would feature 'real girls!'. Four of the cast of twenty came from Crossley and Porter, 'across the moor', to

perform in 'an action-packed drama with romantic scenes', more than enough to entice the Heath boys to fill their school hall. From left to right: Michael Shaw as Dick Dudgeon, the disciple; Helen Andrews as Judith Anderson; and Graham Hyland as the Revd Anderson.

Cricket First XI in the late 1970s, with coach Mr Hobson who left in 1980 to teach in Lesotho. From left to right, back row: Mr Alan Hobson, David Owen, -?-, Michael Brayshaw, Martin Berry, David Stollery, David Marshall (?). Front row: Jack Fielden, Neil Gething, Phil Bates, Richard Hoyle, Michael Berry.

Senior basketball team, c. 1978. Contrary to popular belief, rugby wasn't the only sport played at Heath! Basketball was introduced to the school in about 1968, and in 1972 the *Heathen* reported that the team played sixteen matches, eleven of which they won. Opposing teams included Crossley and Porter School. From left to right, back row: Mr Gordon Stansfield (coach), Nigel Sutcliffe, Stephen Firth, Gary Shackleton. Front row: Neil Gething, George Taylor, Andrew Lucas, Chris Anders (?). Gordon Stansfield transferred to Crossley Heath School, teaching modern foreign languages.

Heath under-fifteen rugby team 1980/81, with coach Mr Rod Kay who saw some of them through to success in the First team. Mr Kay became head of geography in 1983 and continues in that role at Crossley Heath School. From left to right, back row: Steve Blackburn, Paul Bull, Adrian Cocker, Paul Opacic, Nick Tobin, Jonathan Hamer, James Scrimshaw, Peter Ambler, Tahir Younis. Front row: Martin Potts, Robert Stollery, Bryan Butterworth, Michael Hynes, Michael Priestley, Simon Harrison, Dave Collins. Jonathan Hamer and James Scrimshaw went on to play for Bradford Northern (subsequently Bradford Bulls).

Heath's prefects in their maroon blazers with gold braid in 1985. Heath Grammar School managed to avoid closure and J.T. Bunch followed Albert Crosby as twenty-third and final headmaster. He managed the transition of Heath Grammar School to Crossley Heath School and became headmaster of the new entity, following P.F. Barker who was headmaster of Crossley and Porter School. From left to right, back row: R. Birks, P. Russell, R. Fellowes, D. Nicholl, C. Berridge, T. Aziz, N. Burnett, S. Joyce. Front row: A. Atkinson, J. Zaman, N. Tobin, Mr J.T. Bunch, N. Holden, H. Reilly, S. Akhtar.

ALUMNI

A sketchy history of Andrew Watson (back row, centre) can be pieced together from references in the archive material. A BBC Scotland programme was recently made honouring the fact that he was the first black man to play for a senior football team in the UK and the world's first black international football captain. Born in 1857, his early life was spent in British Guiana (now Guyana). He was definitely admitted to Heath Grammar School in August 1866 by Dr Cox, and there is a possibility that he attended and lived at Crossley Orphan Home. Some researchers believe he is to be seen in the *c.* 1865 photograph (see p.42), but this has *never* been verified as fact and his name does not appear in any records. He attended Glasgow University from 1895-1896 and played for Queen's Park, Scotland's oldest football club from 1880-1897. He showed such distinction that he won international honours with Scotland and actually captained the side in 1881 in his first game, which was against England. The school has a replica of his shirt donated by BBC Scotland.

Laurence Sterne (1713-1768), the author of *Tristram Shandy*, was sent to 'a school in Halifax' where he learned Latin and Greek. In his history of Heath Grammar School, 1879, Dr Cox writes, 'Mr Lister, the seventh master, must have the honour of having found out the genius of Laurence Sterne, if tradition is to be depended on, though he could hardly have educated him'. Heath cannot claim beyond doubt that Laurence Sterne attended Heath, for such a claim would be disputed by Hipperholme Grammar School, Halifax. Cox even ponders the possibility that Sterne may have attended both schools. What is certain is that his uncle, Richard Sterne, was a governor of the school and lived at the bottom of Woodhouse Lane, near Sterne Mills and Sterne Bridge.

The end of an era! From left to right are John Allingham, Brian Holloway, Malcolm Bamforth, Russell Smith and John Davey, who are removing the dismantled First World War memorial board from the top corridor of the former Heath School to the new entity, Crossley Heath School, in 1997. The memorial is now mounted on the wall outside Crossley Heath assembly hall. Nearly 300 Old Heathens served in the forces, of whom more than fifty died.

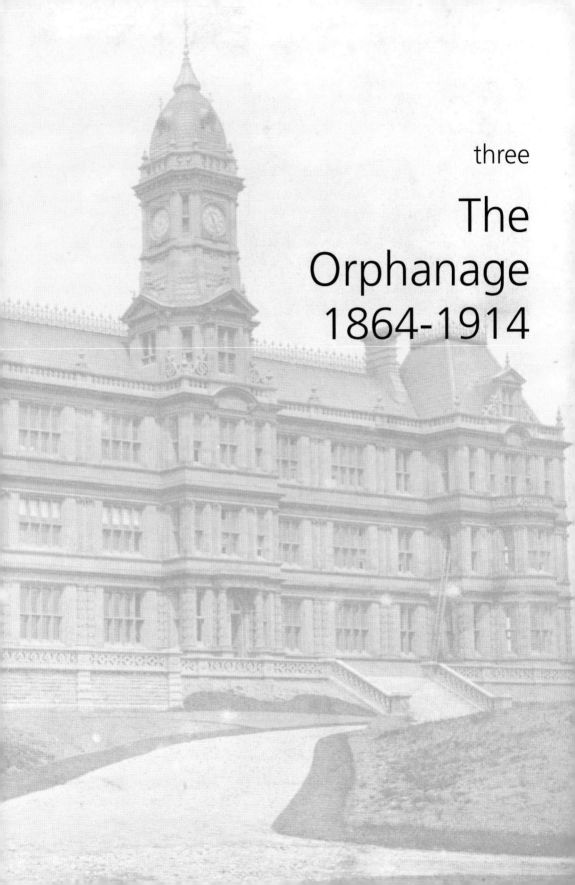

three

The
Orphanage
1864-1914

The Crossley Heath school building owes its existence to the philanthropy of the Crossley brothers, Francis, John and Joseph. In 1857, they formulated a scheme for the establishment of a 'superior college for the district'. Building work began the same year but by 1861 the brothers had decided to establish an 'Orphan Home and School for Boys and Girls'. With the building work complete, the first six orphans, all boys, arrived in June 1864, although there was no official opening ceremony and much internal furnishing work remained to be completed.

The Deed of Foundation was granted a Royal Charter of Incorporation in September 1868. Its fifty-three articles stipulated precisely how the orphanage was to be run by a governing body consisting of three Crossley family governors and fifteen elected governors. Halifax Borough Council elected three of the latter, while various independent non-conformist churches throughout the former West Riding of Yorkshire elected the other twelve. A large endowment fund provided an annual income, which financed the running costs of the orphanage. The size of the fund effectively determined the number of orphans who could be admitted. Donations and subscriptions, including £100 per annum from the industrialist Sir Titus Salt, swelled the endowment fund. By 1874, there were around 250 resident orphans, from all parts of the country, with only twenty per cent from Halifax itself. Many paid fees, up to a maximum of £10 per annum. In summer, annual meetings were held to discuss orphanage business. The proceedings were published in an official report.

These words are taken from a letter written by the Crossley brothers early in 1864, inviting applications for admission to the orphanage.

The school year, consisting of two long terms, ran from January to December, with four weeks of vacation in summer and two at Christmas, an Easter break being introduced later. Orphans could be visited for two (later three) hours on the first Tuesday of each month. There was a small resident teaching staff, headed by the principal. Between late 1864 and early 1910, there were only two principals, Mr Oliver and Mr Barber. A much larger domestic staff numbered over thirty by 1900. The traditional subjects of scripture, reading, writing and arithmetic were emphasised, although all the orphans were also taught geography, drawing, basic natural science and singing. More capable boys were additionally taught Latin, one modern language and more advanced arithmetic, algebra and geometry. At first, girls' education concentrated on needlework and 'useful departments of household service'.

Prior to 1870, education in Britain had been entrusted largely to family and church. That year's Elementary Education Act introduced limited state influence and, in 1871, Mr J.C. Curtis, principal of the Borough Road Training College, London, began annual inspections of the school, stimulating a marked improvement in educational standards within the orphanage. Cambridge Local examinations were introduced in December 1876. In 1877, with more academic subjects available to them, the girls got their own headmistress. There were now effectively two separate schools in one building: the girls' school occupying the south-west side of the building, facing Skircoat Moor Road, and the boys' school the other half.

Departing orphans made their way to all parts of the country, and eventually the world. Such was their fondness for their *alma mater* that when the governors first invited old scholars to attend their annual meeting in 1874, no fewer than ninety responded, starting a tradition of regular reunions which continues today. Sixteen reunions had taken place when, in 1900, the Old Boys' Association was formed, followed some years later by an old girls' equivalent, a merger in 1920 creating the Old Scholars' Association, which remains active today.

In 1887, a Manchester yarn merchant, Thomas Porter, made an endowment of £50,007 on condition that the institution be renamed 'The Crossley and Porter Orphan Home and School', as approved by a supplemental Royal Charter. The extra funding allowed orphan numbers to remain between 240 and 265 until the First World War. It also facilitated the purchase of land opposite the south-west façade and a nearby site, where a sanatorium was built. Scholarships to Bradford Grammar School were introduced, academic standards continuing to improve into the twentieth century.

In 1899, the Board of Education was established and in February 1903 it recognised the combined school as an 'efficient secondary school'. However, annual deficits were incurred from 1901 to 1904, partly because of the higher salaries of better-qualified teachers. General subscriptions fell over eighty-five per cent between 1881 and 1901 and the governors were under pressure to make improvements at the board's request. Staff cuts temporarily restored the financial situation but the monetary pressures of the next two decades would threaten the very existence of the orphanage. Its golden jubilee was nevertheless celebrated in a spirit of optimism over three days at Whitsuntide in 1914, coinciding with the twenty-second old scholars' reunion.

> When the ear heard me, then it blessed me;
> And when the eye saw me, it gave witness to me;
> Because I delivered the poor that cried, and the fatherless, and him that had none to help him.
> The blessing of him that was ready to perish came upon me;
> And I caused the widow's heart to sing for joy.

This passage from the book of Job was quoted in the frontispiece of the annual reports of the orphanage and schools until 1939.

Orphanage founders the Crossley brothers, from left to right: Joseph (26.12.1813-14.9.1868), Francis (26.10.1817-5.1.1872) and John (16.5.1812-16.4.1879), three of the five sons of John and Martha Crossley. John senior, a self-made man, bought a small mill at Dean Clough. In the hands of the three sons, it grew into a large complex, eventually employing over 5,000 people. The brothers' wealth enabled each to live in a large mansion in Halifax – Joseph at Broomfield, Francis at Belle Vue and John at Manor Heath. In common with several other prominent Victorian industrialists, the Crossley brothers gave generously of their wealth for the common good. Francis built and endowed twenty-four almshouses on Margaret Street near Belle Vue, and Joseph built another forty-eight on Arden Road. Francis gave People's Park to Halifax in 1857. The brothers were also major contributors to the construction of Square and Park Congregational churches, but the construction and endowment of the orphanage is considered by many to be their finest act of charity. Both Francis and John were local MPs and Francis was knighted in 1865. He bought the Somerleyton Estate, near Lowestoft, from Samuel Morton Peto in 1862 and his only son, Sir Savile Brinton Crossley, became Lord Somerleyton in 1916. The first orphan, James Labron Plint, regularly saw the three brothers on their visits to the orphanage. He described John as 'tall, straight and very dignified', Joseph as 'rather short and stern looking', and Francis as 'handsome, genial and always kind of jolly'.

The orphanage, shown in 1864, was built on John Crossley's land, 'eight acres, two roods and eight perches' at the top (west) end of Skircoat Moor, later Savile Park. The architect was John Hogg of Halifax, and construction cost around £56,000. 'Of the architecture of the reign of King James I with a mixture of the Italian style', it had a planned capacity for 400 orphans. Behind the main building were separate boys' and girls' playrooms and swimming baths, and ancillary buildings such as the laundry. Around 1883, a two-storey extension was built for the girls' headmistress.

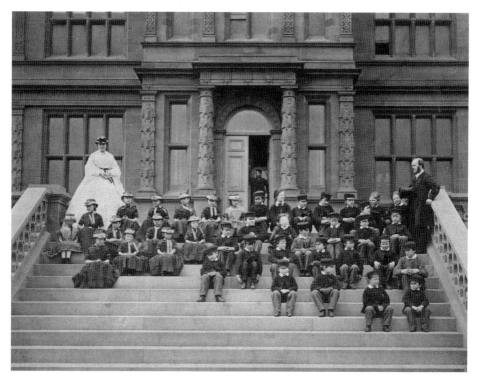

This view of the school on the front steps (*c.* 1865) is the forerunner of hundreds of photographs taken in this familiar setting. Mr Oliver, the principal, and Mrs Smith, the matron resplendent in crinoline, watch over their flock of twenty-six boys and thirteen girls. By the end of 1865, there were sixty-seven orphans in residence. Mrs Smith was succeeded by the principal's wife in 1866.

The first principal was Mr Bithell but only eight boys had been admitted to an incompletely furnished building when Mr Arthur Oliver took over as principal on 15 December 1864. An orphan later wrote of him that 'a better organiser could not have been', while adding 'he ruled rather too much with the rod'. Another commented that Mr Oliver had a 'stern commanding air that struck terror through us', although he was 'strictly impartial and scrupulously fair'. A pious man, he was 'impressive in the pulpit', resorting to 'fire and brimstone' in his sermons. On Sundays, he would march the orphans down to Square Chapel, one-and-a-half miles away, or if the weather was poor, to the nearby King Cross Wesleyan Chapel. After leaving the orphanage in 1872, Mr Oliver became a deacon while running his own educational establishment. He is shown here in the late 1860s with Frank Bainbridge, boy No. 67.

Miss Soul, the first female teacher, shown in the late 1860s with six orphan girls and Mr Oliver's daughters Lizzie and Laura. Lizzie, far right, much later became headmistress of the junior section at Taunton School, where Mr Newport, future Crossley and Porter headmaster, was her colleague from 1899. As Mrs Musgrave of Bradford, she attended the 1940 reunion. She died in 1943 aged eighty-nine.

The number of teaching staff increased gradually as orphan numbers grew. By 1867 there were two assistant masters and two assistant mistresses. Mr Pocklington, shown in 1866, was the first male teacher, described by one boy as 'of a swarthy, forbidding aspect' and 'cynical and cutting both with cane and tongue'. He left at the end of 1867. Note the top hat on the table.

Mr Tozer, a junior master (form II), was well liked by the boys. The orphans had half days on Wednesdays and Saturdays and Mr Tozer would lead mid-week walks to various locations in and around the Calder Valley. A good cricketer and hockey player, he was reported once to have jumped into the swimming bath to save a drowning boy. He left in the early 1870s.

Hockey had been the boys' winter game until the arrival, in August 1876, of Mr J.S. Davidson. A fine footballer himself, Mr Davidson organised the first school soccer and rugby teams, which initially played in the Halifax colours of blue and white. Described as a kindly, earnest, Christian gentleman, Mr Davidson, senior master of forms V and VI, left in 1880, taking a degree at Durham University before becoming ordained in the ministry.

James Labron Plint was the first boy admitted to the orphanage in late June 1864. He left in the summer of 1870, became a seaman and, as third officer, was twice decorated for bravery – for the rescue of a French ship crew in 1879 and for saving a drowning boy at Antwerp the following year. Eventually settling in Liverpool, he visited the orphanage in 1912 and then became intimately associated with all subsequent old scholars' activities in support of the school. He died in 1937. The school uniform included grey trousers and waistcoat, with a dark blue jacket buttoned at the neck. A steel buckle fastened the boots to the ankle. Surprisingly, the uniform was not superseded until the 1920s.

Left: It was naturally common for family groups of orphans to arrive together, the McKenzie sisters, Jane, Ella and Eugenie, being admitted in the 1860s. Eugenie, lower right, appears to have been musically gifted, performing in a piano duet in a children's concert on 29 November 1867. One former girl remembered the orphanage clothes as 'numerous and voluminous'. There were brown dresses in winter and grey ones in summer, with black stockings and elastic-sided boots. For going out, the girls wore jackets and ulsters with hoods attached. There were white straw hats ('pancakes') in summer and black felt and blue velvet ones ('pork-pies') in winter.

Below: Four of the school maids, shown here in the 1860s with an unidentified male member of the domestic staff, possibly 'Jerry' Bloomer, the porter. The laundry baskets are clearly the property of the Crossley Orphan Home.

William Cambridge Barber, FRGS, became principal at the age of thirty-two in July 1872. Born and educated in Gloucester, he qualified at the Borough Road Training College, Isleworth, and was credited with having taught, at elementary level, from the age of fifteen. He had his own school for seven years before taking over at the orphanage. Described as 'a high-minded model churchman and pious scholar', he was also said to have a strong physique and commanding personality, his 'piety and culture inspiring a feeling almost of veneration'. Within a year of his arrival, the school's formal inspector, Mr Curtis, commented that the principal had 'aroused a spirit of vigorous industry throughout the school'. Mr Barber introduced pre-breakfast study periods and applied the same syllabus for both boys and girls, measuring progress with a battery of new examinations, notably the Cambridge Locals from December 1876. Strict discipline was enforced. Mr Curtis was impressed, writing in 1875: 'I can conscientiously speak of it (the school) in terms of warm approval'. Mr Barber taught mathematics, authored several school books and lectured on diverse subjects, including poets, music, birds and glaciers. Two Edison phonographs of his lectures still exist in the archives. He played cello in the Dean Clough Orchestra, was vice-president of the Halifax Choral Society and also president of the Shakespearean Society in Halifax until his death, from a heart attack brought on by pneumonia, in February 1910. A memorial service was held at Halifax Parish Church. The huge funeral cortege consisted of friends and family, the governors, old scholars, teaching and domestic staff and nearly 200 of the orphans. Residents along Free School Lane also paid their respects as the procession passed. Mr Barber was finally laid to rest in Hanwell. A copper and bronze memorial tablet mounted on a marble slab was unveiled in the dining hall on 17 June 1911. In 2006, it adorns the front corridor.

During the 1860s, both boys and girls were divided into four forms. With increasing numbers and Mr Barber's arrival, forms V and VI were created for senior boys, shown in 1874 with Mr Barber (left) and Mr W.J. Hargreaves, assistant master from May 1873 to December 1874. W.H. Breach, second right on the front row, went on to obtain an OBE. In the 1930s, he donated various fives competition prizes.

A February 1874 view of seven senior girls, with two wardrobe staff and, from left to right, seated: Mr John Tuley, Miss Shepherd and Mr Barber. Mr Tuley, 'Clerk to the Board' from 1864 to 1893, was one of the nine founders. While in office, he began the collection of photographic and documentary evidence of the school's activities which eventually grew into today's extensive archive. Miss Shepherd was matron from 1872 until her death from pneumonia in 1887. Nicknamed 'Molly', she had little sympathy for those who complained about the rather spartan meals, regularly meting out a spoonful of brimstone and treacle. Nevertheless, she reportedly displayed kindness to those who fell sick.

Mr Barber with a group of girls and an unidentified female teacher, *c.* 1874. After Mr Barber's arrival in July 1872, the girls were offered a broader range of subjects. For example, by 1876 they were taking examinations in animal physiology and physical geography, and by 1881 they were studying botany.

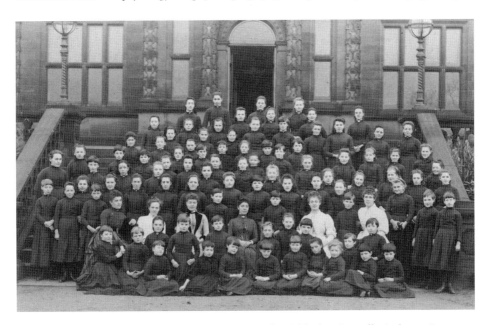

In 1877, a headmistress was first appointed to oversee the girls' education, effectively creating a separate girls' school. By 1889, when this photograph was taken, there were around ninety-five girls in the orphanage. Miss Angela Collins (seated, centre), a former pupil, was appointed headmistress internally in 1880, succeeding Miss Larritt, whose principles she perpetuated. Said to be an excellent teacher, she placed science at the forefront of the girls' curriculum. There were few failures in the Cambridge Local examinations, some of the girls reportedly scoring the highest marks in the country. Miss Collins resigned in 1892 in order to get married.

During the 1880s and 1890s, the girls' school comprised five forms. Apart from the headmistress, there were five resident assistant lady teachers, as shown here in 1889. Piano was taught by a visiting teacher. Staff turnover was much lower than in the boys' school and most lady teachers were former pupils. From left to right: Misses Perry, Metcalfe, Collins (headmistress), Murley, Wheeler and Wilkinson. Georgina Gordon Metcalfe taught at the school from February 1886 until September 1912, including a spell as sixth form mistress. Miss Wilkinson left the school in 1901, returning as matron in 1913.

In the 1890s, the boys' school had six resident assistant teachers, as shown here on the girls' terrace in 1892. Non-resident assistant teachers included Sergeant Boyle, a retired army veteran of the Crimean War, who was visiting drill instructor. From left to right: Messrs Ingham, Lewthwaite, Merrick, Sweetman, Gabbatt, Ovey. Richard Baxter Ingham, or 'Inky', was a favourite with the boys. He had taught in Virginia, USA, and on Sunday afternoons would read from James Fenimore Cooper and recount his own experiences. In 1895, he returned to America, where he taught for many more years.

Organised school cricket began in the early 1870s. This is the 1874 school team with Mr J.H. Dove (assistant teacher 1873-1876). The light blue cricket cap was then the only item of cricket clothing, although flannel suits were worn by the mid-1890s. Despite playing in school uniform, the 1870s teams were reckoned to be among the best in Halifax. By the end of the 1880s, the sport had been organised into a club, with a captain and vice-captain. Before Broomfield became available in 1914, various grounds used included Copley and King Cross.

By the season of 1888/9, the football club, playing both soccer and rugby, had been established formally, with the enthusiastic Mr Ingham as secretary. Initially hampered by having to play in the heavy, clasp-fastened school shoes, the rugby team received boots the following year. Shirts were initially chocolate and cream. The 1889/90 rugby team is shown with Mr Ingham and Mr Barber. The reserves are in school uniform. E.J. Bryer, the captain, is holding the ball. The boy with his hand on his shoulder is Herbert Holt, who went on to become a vice-president of the Old Crossleyans RUFC and was also treasurer of the Jubilee Playing Field and First World War memorial funds.

Above: In the early years, with so many children in close proximity on a rather basic diet, in a building with inefficient heating, infectious diseases were relatively common. Unoccupied dormitories were used as makeshift isolation wards, although as early as 1878 the governors were hoping 'to erect a detached infirmary or sanatorium'. In 1888, a site was secured on the opposite side of Skircoat Moor Road but, ironically, building was delayed in 1890 by a serious outbreak of diphtheria, which killed two girls and necessitated an expensive evacuation and a rebuilding of the school's sewerage system. The following year, the incomplete sanatorium was forced into use by outbreaks of scarlet fever and measles. Despite its usefulness, the sanatorium eventually proved a drain on limited resources, at a time of improving health and the availability of the Halifax Royal Infirmary. With the school in serious post-war debt, the sanatorium was sold in 1923. The building, latterly known as Horsfall House, was demolished in 2001. This is an 1899 view of the sanatorium entrance from Skircoat Moor Road.

Left: In one of the burial grounds of the King Cross Methodist Church is the orphanage grave, still surviving in 2006 albeit considerably overgrown. Over some forty years, about twenty-five orphans died and the grave records the deaths of six of them between the ages of seven and sixteen. Causes of death typified the diseases, such as scarlet fever, diphtheria and tuberculosis, suffered by children of the day. In 1872, even smallpox was detected in one of the lodges but fortunately it did not enter the main building. The headstone reads: 'Sacred to the Memory of CHILDREN who have died in the CROSSLEY ORPHAN HOME and SCHOOL'. Adjacent is the grave of Mr and Mrs Oliver.

Sick rooms dealt with minor illness. Ringworm, for example, which was regarded as 'really troublesome', was fairly common in the 1900s, often necessitating months of isolation and treatment with ointments. The small sick room, shown here in 1899, was located on the top floor of the girls' side. Converted for botany in 1920, it eventually became a chemistry laboratory. In 1910, £14 18s 6d was spent on X-ray apparatus, to be used in the

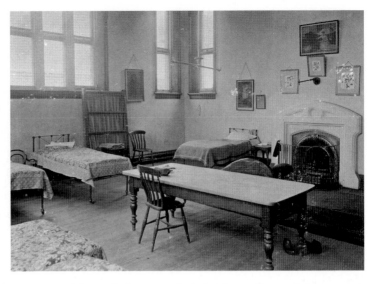

treatment of ringworm! Other rooms used for medical purposes included the small ground-floor room, off the boys' stairs, where the visiting dentist held surgery twice monthly between the wars.

With 260 orphans, the laundry was a busy place around 1900. Located across the courtyard behind the school, it was equipped with stone cisterns, drums and a centrifugal wringer, described as 'all in constant use'. There was a central drying chamber and adjacent ironing room, equipped with an automatic steam mangle. The laundry was completely overhauled and re-equipped during 1920-1. With its hot, steamy atmosphere, it was a welcome refuge on cold days. Note the belt-driven machinery in this undated view.

Domestic staff, thirty-one of whom are shown here around 1900, far outnumbered the teaching staff. The female staff included the matron and her assistant, two nurses, a wardrobe staff of six, two kitchen maids, two pantry maids and various house and laundry maids. Miss Esberger, fifth from left in the second row, was matron from 1899 to 1907. Her assistant and successor, Miss Tyers, sits to her right. On the matron's left is one of the nurses; the other is sitting on the far left in the front row. Second from left in the second row is Mrs Kirk, the boys' head wardrobe keeper, with one of her assistants to her left. Sixth from left in the third row is Miss Florence 'Florrie' Tomlin, the popular cook from 1899 to 1923. She would give the girls cookery lessons on Saturday afternoons, followed by a nourishing school-kitchen tea. From left to right in the back row are: the baker, sweeper, caretaker, tailor, engineer and two cobblers, father and son. The bakery was located in the basement below the kitchen and was capable of turning out 175 loaves each day. Boys on boot-cleaning duty next door were not averse to raiding the bakery. Mr Wright Whitwam, the caretaker, lived in the front (south) lodge, while the back (north) lodge was occupied by Mr Edgar Riley, school engineer from 1878 to 1911. Apart from maintaining the school's heating system, he reared pigs in a small enclosure off the girls' playground. Naturally enough, the pigs' occasional illicit liberation caused the boys much amusement. Thomas Sutcliffe, cobbler, worked at the school from 1874 to 1909 while his son Herbert, 'young cobbie', died in 1929 with forty-one years' service behind him.

Opposite above: Located at the back of the building next to the tailor's room, the workroom is shown on 10 August 1899. The four sewing machines were used by practical dressmakers who made most of the children's clothing. As girls became more adept at needlework, they were entrusted with some of this work. The 1904 annual report states that the girls made 433 garments and mended 9,270! Note the overhead gas jets used for lighting. In 2006, this room is part of the learning resource centre.

As 'general factotum', Mr Wright Whitwam had a wide variety of duties. In the 1880s he would organise the erection of a massive dining hall gallery, upon which all the children sat for annual oral examinations in front of the staff and governors. More mundane duties included supervising the boys of the 'industrial squad' in daily boot cleaning. At the boys' weekly hot baths he was tasked with rubbing soap into their scalps and rinsing off the suds with a bucket of water, as shown here *c.* 1908. He was presented with an inscribed gold watch on retirement in November 1917, after thirty-three-and-a-half years of service.

The reception room by the front entrance, shown here in 1899, was where the board of governors met and where the secretary worked. Portraits of the founders hung on the walls, with large boards recording donations and bequests. Other records included leaving portrait photographs of all boys and girls. During 1864, when the building's internal furnishings were incomplete, the first boys were taught in this room, sleeping in the dormitory overhead. The Old Scholars' committee meetings were later held here. The room was converted to a library and sixth-form study in 1952. In 2006, it is the A2 classroom.

Succeeding Miss Wayte as headmistress in 1897 and pictured here in September 1899, Miss Dora Knight was formerly at Dulwich High School. A capable administrator, she was said to have an 'orderly mind and generous heart'. She once treated the girls to a trip to Hardcastle Crags on her birthday. Apparently convinced of the benefits of exercise and fresh air, she organised walks for the girls on Saturday afternoons and a fellow staff member recalled her touring the dormitories at night, opening windows with a croquet mallet. Retiring to the family home in Petersfield in 1913, she died there in 1940, aged eighty-one.

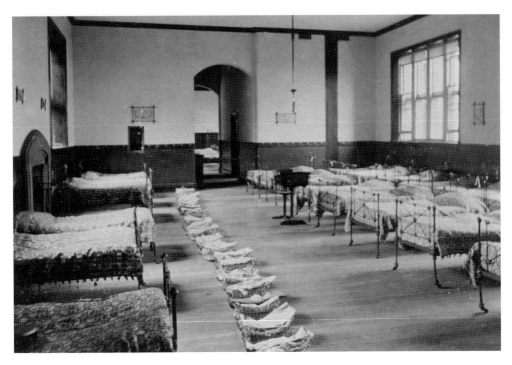

The girls' middle school dormitory, shown in the late nineteenth century. Wire baskets were used for clothes. The window of a cubicle bedroom, provided for mistresses to overlook the dormitories, may be seen to the left of the archway. Between the wars, the girls' dormitories had names. Younger girls slept in 'The Zoo', while senior girls had individual cubicles in top-floor rooms, including the 'Dovecot', 'Rookery', 'Crow's Nest' and 'Eagle's Nest'. The first-floor room shown here became 'Vanity Fair'. Converted to a classroom in 1942, it is used for art in 2006.

The girls' playroom, shown here in September 1900, was initially used as a joiner's shop as internal furnishing of the building continued. 'Joint use' finished only in the early 1870s. The large cupboard along the wall contained numbered compartments for shoes and bedroom slippers. All of an orphan's clothes bore his or her number. Assemblies were also held in this room. Note the tiered benches. On the right is the door leading to the girls' swimming bath, which was closed after the First World War.

Two large ground-floor schoolrooms, either side of the dining hall, each measured sixty by thirty feet. In the 1860s, as numbers increased, four forms were created by dividing each large schoolroom with blackboards. Shown here in summer 1899 are parts of forms II, III and IV on the boys' side. Around 1912, several smaller rooms were created here using glass partitions, the area becoming known as the 'glasshouse'. In 2006, this is the school dining room. The current staffroom occupies much of the former girls' schoolroom. The main corridors adjacent to these rooms were created only after the Second World War. Electric lighting in classrooms was provided from 1920.

The boys' fifth and sixth forms each had a room along the corridor from the large schoolroom. This, currently A35, is the larger sixth form room, c. 1902. Orphans progressed according to their scholastic ability. One claimed to have made it to the sixth form before his tenth birthday, staying there until the leaving age of fifteen and sitting the same Cambridge Local examinations repeatedly. This was also the examination room. The cabinets housed academic materials and Mr Barber's cane, which was brandished on a daily basis. Early science demonstrations were held on the purpose-built table.

The 1902/3 soccer team, captained by H. Shaw. The school's football club played both rugby and soccer but rugby faded before the First World War, possibly because boys left at fifteen, giving opposing teams an unfair size advantage. In 1892, annual 'past v. present' football fixtures began between the school team and old boys. In 1912, both home and away games, played in October and December at Exley, were soccer. Autumn 1919 saw the last full soccer fixture list, after which the school adopted rugby as the boys' winter game.

Two lawn tennis courts were located among the trees in front of the school. In the nineteenth century the game was popular with the staff, as shown here, c. 1886. From left to right are: Miss Wilkinson, Mr Cockett, Miss Collins (headmistress), Mr Westgate, Miss Metcalfe, Miss Murley, Mr Blencairn, Mr Perry, –?–, Mr Harrison, Miss Waterhouse. In 1921, the CPS Tennis Club was formed, the courts being run by the Old Scholars' Association which had reconditioned them.

Music was taught from the earliest days of the orphanage, usually by visiting teachers. Mr Herman Van Dyk taught piano, violin and singing from July 1895 to December 1922. Born in Leeuwarden, Holland, Mr Van Dyk settled in Yorkshire in the early 1890s, becoming conductor of the Halifax Orchestral Society in 1901. Both he and his wife (pictured) were accomplished pianists. Mr Van Dyk also taught conversational German and his nephew, Louis, was modern languages master at the school in the early 1920s.

From the 1870s, there developed a tradition of winter concerts, plays and sketches to provide entertainment for the boarders. In February 1912, the sixth form boys put on a production of *A Midsummer Night's Dream*. The sets, including the splendid Palace of Theseus and Quince's house, with the acropolis and setting sun in the background, were built by Mr Rucklidge, assisted by F.C. Leach. The boys filled all the roles creditably, although breaking voices and masculine shape made for awkwardness in a number of female roles. The successful show raised some £15.

Right: Sir Herbert Read (1893-1968), perhaps the most illustrious of the orphanage alumni, was born near Kirkbymoorside in north Yorkshire and was admitted on his father's death in 1904. This is his leaving portrait, taken in December 1908. He later studied at Leeds University, serving with the Yorkshire Regiment in the First World War and being awarded the DSO and MC. Appointed assistant keeper of the Victoria and Albert Museum in 1922, his subsequent career as a poet, essayist and critic produced over sixty published books. Knighted in 1953 for services to literature, he was also guest speaker at school speech days.

Below: Boys and girls, seated separately, took their meals together in the dining hall. The nineteenth-century diet was described as 'decidedly spartan'. In the kitchen, large porridge boilers catered for breakfast. The milk was cold, occasionally with ice on it. Bread was another staple and orphans found it useful for cleaning plates between the main lunch course and pudding. Resourceful boys took to supplementing their diet by raiding the teachers' dining area at night for the plentiful leftovers. Redecorated for the golden jubilee celebrations in June 1914, with boys allowed to sit alongside girls for the first time, the dining hall was also used for all important meetings and performances, including annual meetings of the governing body, musical concerts, lectures and dramatic performances.

The golden jubilee celebrations began with a service at Square Chapel on Whit Sunday, 31 May 1914. The next day the main programme began with lunch, with children accommodated in the dining hall and adults in a marquee. The annual meeting followed. Tea and further meetings preceded an impromptu 'social and dance', which lasted until *Auld Lang Syne* at 9.30 p.m. Most of the old boys in the traditional photograph are shown wearing special bronze jubilee medals. Fifth from left in the front row is James Labron Plint, boy No. 1. He won the veterans' 100 yards next day, at the age of fifty-eight!

The old girls' group at the golden jubilee reunion on 1 June 1914. Lady Crossley had distributed the jubilee medals to all scholars and staff on behalf of the governors. Each child also received a tin of Mackintosh's Toffee de Luxe, a gift from the Old Boys' jubilee fund. Next day, sports were held at Broomfield, with lunch provided by the governors and tea by the Old Boys. The younger girls then performed *White Magic*, a play arranged by Miss Dale, the headmistress, and Miss Croft. The obligatory speeches were followed by *God Save The King*, which concluded the celebrations.

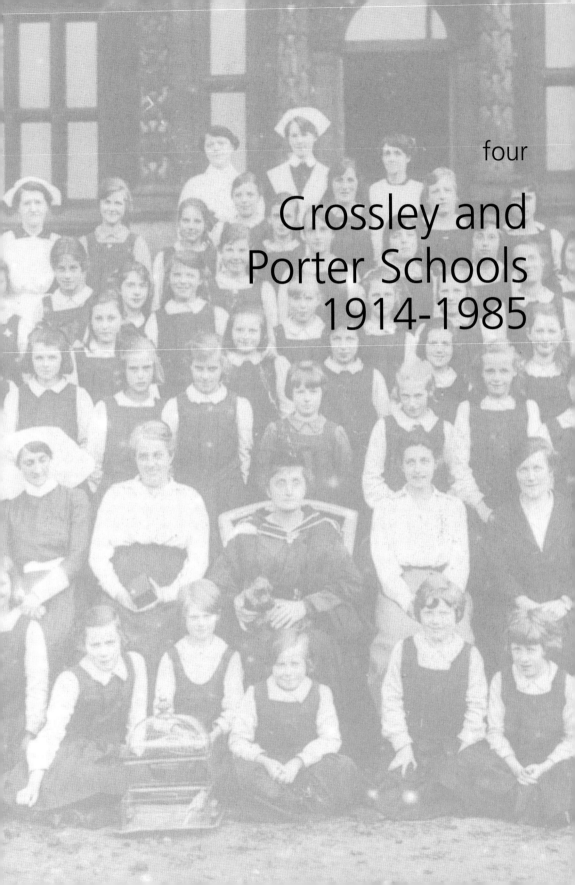

four

Crossley and
Porter Schools
1914-1985

At the golden jubilee celebrations in June 1914, the schools were looking forward optimistically, with new classrooms being opened and science laboratories planned. The Old Boys' Association had donated new playing fields at Broomfield. In the summer, extensive improvements to the heating, lighting and sanitation delayed the start of term until October. However, with the onset of war everyday costs escalated, subscriptions dropped again and annual deficits of around £1,000 became the norm. The governors decided neither to decrease numbers nor to increase fees, in order to spare orphans and their families further hardship, and Francis Crossley's son, Sir Savile Brinton Crossley, Lord Somerleyton from 1916, pledged an extra £650 per annum from the Crossley family.

Following the 1918 Education Act, the schools became recognised grant-earning schools, and were renamed 'The Crossley and Porter Schools, Halifax', as approved by the Board of Education and confirmed by an Act of Parliament in 1919. The governing body now comprised four foundation governors and fifteen representative governors, the latter including five elected by Halifax Council and several more elected by Yorkshire municipal councils. The 1918 Act had raised school leaving age to fourteen and the governors planned to provide education up to the age of eighteen. Fee-paying day pupils were admitted for the first time, with 175 attending daily by 1925, the number of boarders having declined to just 105.

Sir Savile Brinton Crossley, son of Sir Francis Crossley, became, in 1916, The Right Hon. Lord Somerleyton, P.C., G.C.V.O.

John William and Mary Ann Standeven.

Nevertheless, the deficit exceeded £16,000 in 1922, despite an increase in boarders' fees to £40. A diamond jubilee festival was planned, with the sole objective of clearing the debt. All those connected with the schools – staff, pupils, old scholars, local businesses and individuals – rose magnificently to the appeal for funds. Sale of the sanatorium realised £3,010, planned improvements were postponed and the four-day festival in July-August 1924 brought the appeal to a successful close, the debt being cleared by the year's end. In response to this, Mr John William Standeven gave an endowment of £10,000 in memory of his late wife, Mary Ann. Income from the endowment was used to lower boarders' fees.

Ironically, as the country headed toward industrial strife and the Depression, the schools entered a relatively prosperous period. Two new wings were constructed, along with fives courts and a manual workshop. The girls began cookery, laundry, pottery and gardening. Mr Newport and Miss Dale had divided both schools into houses and inter-house sporting competitions flourished. By 1930, both schools had small sixth forms, studying for the Higher School Certificate. A growing number of school societies catered for extra-curricular interests. Scout, Cub, Guide and Brownie groups were formed. Overall physical fitness was improved by the introduction of twice-weekly compulsory games for all boys. A doctor oversaw general health and a dentist visited every fortnight. By the summer of 1939, 3,036 boarders – 1,975 boys and 1,061 girls – had been admitted since 1864.

The Second World War again disrupted school life. As was the case during the First World War, male staff joined the armed forces and boarders were evacuated to local families. Remaining male staff became air wardens and special constables, and a school cadet force was established. The 1944 Act abolished the Board of Education, designated a minister of education to oversee Local Education Authorities (LEAs) and made secondary education compulsory. The schools became voluntary controlled secondary (grammar) schools, with

Girls of the lower sixth domestic science group with their 1964 centenary cake.

a governing body consisting of five foundation governors and ten representative governors, the latter appointed by the LEA. This arrangement abolished junior sections and fees, the junior section duly closing in 1947 with boarding in the main school building being officially discontinued. The Parents' Association had been formed in the uncertain climate of 1945 and, over subsequent decades, it provided valuable social and fund-raising support for the school.

In 1948, with the family's agreement, the Standeven endowment was used to purchase two new hostels for boarders near Broomfield. The former Ravenswood was renamed Standeven House in memory of Mrs Standeven. It could accommodate sixteen boys and nearby Crossley House (formerly The Gleddings) had room for sixteen girls. The hostels never reached full capacity and closed in 1961, when the last boarders left. The Gleddings was sold and Standeven House was converted for use as a pavilion by the Old Scholars' Association, whose members had extended and developed the adjacent playing fields.

Still with separate heads, the boys' and girls' schools celebrated their centenary together in 1964 and, with everyday cooperation increasing, they were officially merged, under one head, on 1 January 1968. Changes in society in general and education in particular affected the grammar school, although it survived the move toward comprehensive education. However, falling school rolls and limits on public finance highlighted an over-provision of grammar school places in Calderdale. Accordingly, in 1985 the Crossley and Porter School was merged with Heath to form the Crossley Heath School.

In 1910, George Bernard Newport was appointed headmaster from a list of over 150 applicants, six days short of his thirty-fourth birthday. He had graduated in science from Sidney Sussex College, Cambridge in 1898 and had then taught at Taunton School from 1899, becoming senior house master. An accomplished sportsman, he had played football and cricket for Somerset, having also played in hockey trials. An energetic moderniser, Mr Newport was to oversee the transformation of the schools from their Victorian orphanage roots to modern secondary schools, admitting day pupils in the wake of the Fisher Act in 1918. His achievements were the greater for having been effected against the background of the First World War and the straitened financial circumstances which prevailed for many years thereafter. He was responsible for developing systematic teaching of science subjects, establishing fully-equipped chemistry and physics laboratories. In the post-war years, with the raising of the school's leaving age to eighteen, he developed a modern sixth form, which studied for the Higher School Certificate. He also introduced the house system and encouraged extra-curricular interests, leading to the formation of several societies, including the Scientific, and the Debating and Dramatic Societies. As District Scoutmaster, he played a leading role in the successful development of the school's Scouts and Cubs. Affectionately nicknamed 'Guv', he had a profoundly humanising influence on the school and worked enthusiastically to promote and strengthen ties with old scholars. Mr Newport retired in 1941, being succeeded by John Stanley Bolton.

In August 1913, Mary Elizabeth Dale, a graduate of Dublin University, took over as headmistress of the girls' school, having spent ten years at Kendal High School. Along with Mr Newport, she is credited with the modernisation of the schools, keenly supporting the house system, which she believed would encourage individuals to make a contribution to the community. She believed that interest was a better motive than compulsion for learning and was against favouring the brightest girls at the expense of the others, reportedly discontinuing the giving of prizes – a move described as 'extreme' by some at the time. Resigning through ill health in the winter of 1929/30, she kept in touch for many years thereafter, notably via *The Crossleyan* magazine. Miss Dale died in 1963 and, during the centenary celebrations the following year, a plaque was unveiled in her memory, bearing the fitting tribute 'Happiness is a great love and much serving'.

The girls' school and teaching staff in July 1919, just before admission of the first 'day bugs', as fee-paying day girls became known. There were seventy girl boarders on this date. Note the girls' new uniform of a navy blue tunic and blouse, replacing the tight-fitting green frocks and aprons which had been so unpopular. From left to right, the second row staff include: 4th, Miss Wilkinson (matron), 5th, Miss Dale (headmistress) in a mortar board, 8th, Miss Croft, 9th, Miss Cartwright.

In May 1915, four girls found a hoard of Roman coins among the rocks below Albert Promenade. Eventually numbering 1,075, the coins were presented to the Halifax Corporation. Described in the *Yorkshire Archaeological Journal*, most of the coins dated from AD 330 onwards. In recognition of their find, the girls received a certificate with the borough seal, as well as a few of the coins. Left to right, back: Lilian Nicholl, Nancy Berry. Front: Amy Rothwell, Gwendoline Evans.

From 1864 to 1941, a matron controlled domestic arrangements, including catering, nursing in sickness and inspection of clothing. Miss E.R. Wilkinson, a pupil from 1875 to 1883 and then teacher until 1901, was the eighth matron, appointed to succeed Miss Tyers early in 1913. After training in nursing at Bradford Royal Infirmary and graduating with a gold medal in 1904, she had worked as nurse and matron in various locations until returning. Respected as very competent in her work, her generous and warm-hearted nature endeared her to everyone. At Easter 1924 she developed pneumonia, which caused her death on 21 May, aged just fifty-six.

Following the founding of the Scout movement in 1908, the school troop, the 5th Halifax, was formed by Mr Newport before the First World War. After the war, school Cub, Guide and Brownie groups were also started. In June 1921, the Crossley Boy Scouts and Cubs took first prize in the Halifax Royal Infirmary procession. The Scout movement's founder and Chief Scout, Sir Robert Baden-Powell, made a lightning inspection visit on the evening of 9 July 1921 and addressed the gathered crowd on the terrace at the east corner of the building. Scout dens were located in the basement at the front of the building.

The Scouts camped near Bolton Abbey before the First World War and at Broomfield in the 1920s, as shown here with Mr Woodhead (centre left) and Mr Place, at Whitsuntide in 1923. Later, summer camps were held further afield, St Malo being a regular destination. In the 1930s, a general school camp was held annually at Bigbury-on-Sea in Devon. During the First and Second World Wars, boys and girls attended harvest camps. In October 1943, two squads of boys camped with Mr Margerison at Healaugh near Tadcaster. The 1,000 tons of potatoes they lifted in four weeks was hailed as a record in the national press.

Right: Alfred E. Mander arrived as form V master in August 1903, becoming form VI master in 1906. In 1910, he became acting headmaster between Mr Barber's death and Mr Newport's arrival. He was commissioned as lieutenant in the 4th West Riding in 1914. Wounded three times, he returned to the front as captain and adjutant and fell at Paschendaele on 9 October 1917. His name is included on the wall at Tyne Cotte Cemetery, Belgium, for those without a known grave. He was one of hundreds of old boys who fought for their country, notably in the Boer War and the First and Second World Wars. On 23 October 1920, a roll of honour was unveiled to those who fell in the First World War. The cenotaph opposite the front entrance was formally dedicated the same day.

Below: At the 1914 golden jubilee reunion, the Old Boys' Association had donated the new playing fields at Broomfield, which were bought using money raised by the Association.
After the First World War, the Association again began raising funds for a war memorial scheme, of which the roll of honour and cenotaph were two elements. A pavilion at Broomfield completed the scheme. Delayed by the high cost of building post-war, it was finally presented to the governors on 11 December 1926. Shown here on 20 May 1929, the pavilion was dismantled to make way for the levelled and enlarged main rugby pitch, *c.* 1956. By 1964, the purchase of intervening land had linked the original playing fields with Standeven House, which became the new pavilion.

In the 1900s, the Board of Education specified the need for science laboratories. One boy had apparently been refused a job because he lacked practical skills in chemistry. By 1908, Mr Barber had obtained some basic instruments and apparatus and had begun practical physics demonstrations. In 1919, a chemistry laboratory (pictured) was opened in the old 'East' classroom at the corner of the building on the ground floor. A second, smaller laboratory was also opened next to it for chemistry and physics, with equipment installed in 1923.

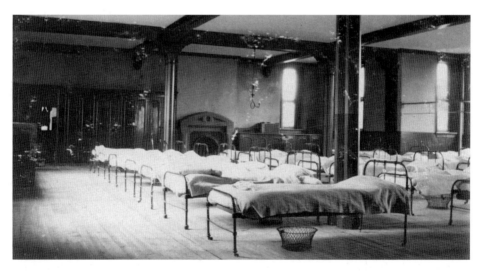

In the inter-war period, the boys' dormitories were allocated by house. The first-floor No. 50 (Spartan) dormitory, shown here in 1921, became the upper hall during the Second World War, and was converted into classrooms in 1947. In 2006 it is part of the English department. Under Mr Barber's strict rule, the boys were put to bed 'by machinery'. Each dormitory had a senior boy as sentinel, who would shout out numbers from one to twelve. Number one was the order to kneel by the bedside, two to place wire baskets on beds, three to place clothes in baskets and so on. A distant twelve finally allowed chilled orphans to get into bed.

From the 1860s, boys and girls had separate pools. The girls' pool was converted into music rooms after the First World War. This is the boys' pool in the early 1920s, looking toward the deep end. It is reputedly one of the oldest non-municipal swimming pools in the country. Note the small diving stand, installed in 1911. The boys held swimming finals and displays in this small bath until 1952. However, the main purpose of the pool has always been to teach swimming skills. In the 1870s, older boys took this upon themselves by simply throwing the younger ones in at the deep end and leaving them to get out as best they could!

The dining hall, as laid out for a special occasion in 1929. Note the stained-glass skylights. Accounts from the 1930s indicate that boys and girls still sat at separate tables for regular meals. Food was set upon trestle tables at the far end, having arrived from the kitchens through the door, appropriately topped with the Crossley family motto *Omne bonum ab alto*, meaning 'All good things come from above'. Serving girls at the trestle tables were supervised by Miss Seed, the matron. The school grace, 'The Lord is good to all', was sung before the meal.

In the 1920s, the girls' school choir regularly entered the secondary school choir section of the Halifax Musical Festival, winning in 1922, 1924 and 1927. The November 1924 winners are shown here with Miss Amy Thompson, modern languages mistress from 1920 to 1936, who trained and conducted them.

A highlight of 1924 was the girls' school production of *The Unknown Warrior's Vision*, a play written and produced by Miss Alice Croft, the senior mistress, who taught history from 1914 to 1930. Appropriately, the play was first performed on Armistice Day after months of preparation, with a cast of over eighty. The Unknown Warrior is universal and eternal, as epitomised in his last words: 'Greater than death is that for which we died'. The play raised £100, facilitating the purchase of a pottery kiln, weaving looms and wood carving tools for the girls' use.

The girls' school teaching staff in January 1928. From left to right, back row: Misses M.G. Herbert, ? Ramstedt, A. Wilman, E. Wishart, ? Holdimann. Front row: Misses A. Thompson, A. Croft, M.E. Dale (headmistress), A.S. Cartwright, N.G. Oakley. Miss Herbert taught geography and history from 1927 to 1950, eventually becoming senior mistress. Miss Cartwright took charge of the lower school in

1916 and also taught elocution, drawing and needlework to the upper school. Ill health caused her premature retirement in 1933. Miss Norah Oakley taught English and Latin from 1926 to 1947.

The masters in 1929. From left to right, back row: A.R. Smith, T.M. Umpleby (visiting), T. Newboult (visiting), S.A. Lebern, W.J. Margerison, W.A. Rucklidge. Front row: C.M. Hanson, J.S. Bolton, G.B. Newport (headmaster), C.H. Place, E.J. Harrison. Mr Bolton arrived as an orphan in 1910, winning a scholarship to Taunton School and graduating from Sidney Sussex, Cambridge. He returned to teach mathematics in 1924, succeeding Mr Newport as headmaster in 1941. Mr Margerison taught English and history. Under his guidance, the Wolf Cubs won the prize for best pack in the Halifax Association several times in the 1930s. Mr Rucklidge taught chemistry and was very active in the scientific society for many years.

The school, as seen from Wainhouse Tower on the evening of 18 July 1928, with the Yorkshire Show in the background on Savile Park. Several developments were imminent on this side of the school. The boys' playground would be asphalted for the first time the following year. Until the 1890s, the boys had cultivated small plots of land by the perimeter wall. At the bottom of the playground stands the new manual workshop, created by the boys themselves by walling off a section of the covered play shed, erected in 1892. Behind the remaining open section of the shed, the fives courts are under construction. Site preparation has not yet begun on the new wings, although both would open within two years. A netball and two tennis courts have been provided on the girls' side but there are no tennis courts yet on the boys' side. The two-storey extension built for the girls' headmistress in the 1880s may be seen between the main building and the girls' gymnasium. The laundry is sandwiched between buildings which originally housed the boys' and girls' pools, although the latter was already closed in 1928. In 1864, the orphanage had stood in open country, one-and-a-half miles from the centre of Halifax. As the area became more built-up, orphanage boys would come into contact with local boys, whom they called 'little Bills'. After the admission of day pupils, the term 'Bill' was adopted for first form boys, with 'Jennies' being the girls' equivalent. Note the shadow cast on the right by the tower, built in 1874.

On 29 July 1930 the two-storey new wings were opened, the boys' side shown here under construction in December 1929. When it opened, there was a library on the ground floor, with music practice rooms and a masters' common room upstairs. To the right are the two fives courts, completed in late 1928. The courts gradually fell into disrepair and were eventually demolished to make way for the new technology building, opened in 2002. The girls' side new wing comprised an art room, a library and two new classrooms, including one for the small sixth form.

Manual instruction in woodwork was started c. 1906, initially using the Haugh Shaw school workshop. Metalwork was included after the First World War. In 1926, Crossley and Porter's own manual workshop was built by the boys themselves, supervised by Mr J.P. Gowland who was art and manual work instructor. After being fitted out with woodwork benches and two lathes, it opened in September 1927. Mr Newport stated that 'the boys should be proud of their achievement'. In the 1950s, the workshop was extended and modernised, incorporating a drawing office and metalwork shop.

Left: Miss Richardson was born at Collingham Bridge near Wetherby, graduating from Leeds University with a BA (Hons) in history in 1920. She taught history at Tamworth Girls' High School, being promoted to second mistress in 1924. Succeeding Miss Dale in March 1930, she chose to continue her predecessor's methods, introducing changes gradually. In addition to teaching history and scripture, 'Ricky', as she was known to the girls, encouraged the performance of plays, such an important part of girls' school activities in the 1930s. In common with the rest of her staff and boarders, she had to vacate the building in 1939, working tirelessly to find the girls alternative local accommodation. Miss Richardson made countless friends while at the school and maintained a keen interest in it after retiring in 1951.

Below: In the 1920s, girls' games included tennis, hockey, netball, badminton, swimming and even cricket. Lacrosse was introduced with the arrival of Miss McConnell in the 1928/9 season. The following season was the last for hockey as the main winter game. In the early years, no Halifax schools played lacrosse and it was difficult to find fixtures. The 1931 team are, from left to right, standing: Miss McConnell, G. Backhouse, M. Robinson, J. Brearley, B. Earnshaw. Kneeling: H. Winter, W. Tanner, K. Goodfellow, M. Sykes, F. Rawson. Sitting: D. Howarth, J. Prescott. Ironically, hockey was reintroduced from 1976.

Right: Many extra subjects were added in the 1920s and group hobbies were encouraged, with the formation of several clubs and societies. In 1925, the girls' school bought a kiln and pottery classes began. These were taught to form IV once a week by Miss Cartwright. Pottery proved very popular and many extra hours were spent in the basement room, shown here in July 1930. Completed work was displayed for many years at annual meetings, along with

girls' weaving and boys' art and woodwork. In 1963, after a long period of disuse, the old pottery room was adapted for the photographic society's meetings.

Below: In the 1920s and '30s, the annual meeting was usually held on the last Tuesday in July. Apart from the official reports and prize-giving on what was termed 'speech day', the boys and girls provided programmes of entertainment. The girls of the lower school are shown giving a display of 'Aesthetic Dances' on the south lawn, after tea on 30 July 1929. These displays were clearly popular and were expanded during the 1930s to include the middle and senior schools, who performed 'English and Country Dancing'. Other entertainments included choral performances, boys' swimming displays and the presentation of short sketches in the hall.

In March 1919, at the invitation of old boy Herbert Goodall, those of his fellows who had served in the armed forces during the First World War dined at the Old Cock Hotel. Thus began an annual old scholars' tradition. In this view, dated 10 March 1933, Mr and Mrs Goodall are on Mr Newport's left. Miss Richardson is third on his right. In 2005, the Old Scholars' Association held its annual Christmas dinner at Standeven House.

The Old Crossleyans RUFC was founded in August 1923. From the earliest days, senior boys turned out for the old scholars' team, which quickly found success. It became the only unbeaten team in Yorkshire in 1924/5, winning twenty-two and drawing two matches. A later Old Crossleyans team, captained by J.S. Bolton, is shown outside the Broomfield pavilion in January 1932. 'Egg' Bolton had managed a few appearances for the Old Crossleyans in their first season, while also representing Sidney Sussex, Cambridge. The following year, at stand-off half, he was the team's top scorer with 107 points in their unbeaten season.

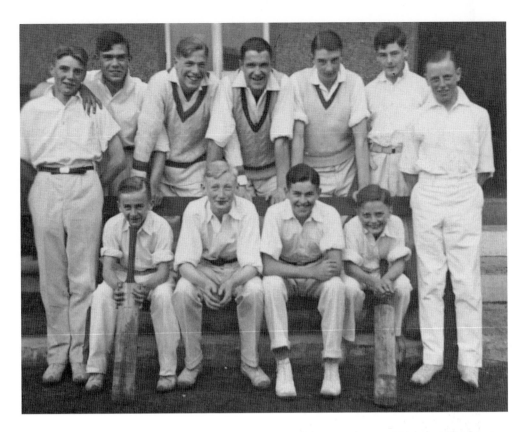

Above: The 1933 school cricket team. From left to right, back row: F. Brennand, H. Barker, E. Stocks, V.W. Rowlands (captain), J.W. Carter, H. Goodfellow, D. Harrison. Front row: W. Baser, D. Nicholl, R. Ullyott, E. Bertelsen. Nicholl set a new record for wickets taken – seventy-one in eighteen matches – in what was otherwise an indifferent season for the team. Carter went on to lead the 1936 team, which won fourteen and drew two of its sixteen matches, the captain averaging 39 and scoring 104 not out against Rishworth School.

Right: Rugby fives was played at both house and school level from 1929. This is the 1934 school team. From left to right, back row: N. Patterson, J.W. Carter, as one pair. Front row: E. Bertelsen, J.W. Rowlands, as the other pair. Bertelsen was a precocious talent, reaching the final of the senior fives competition the previous year, while winning the junior competition. He later set a record of 98/100 on the school rifle range. 'Snoop' Carter was an all-round sportsman, captaining the Old Crossleyans rugby team in 1937/8. Tragically, both he and Rowlands were killed in the Second World War.

Reunions began as early as 1874 when the governors invited old scholars to their annual meeting. The dining hall was used for the main business meeting and a marquee was erected for the provision of lunch and tea. Located for many years on the boys' side, opposite the large schoolroom, the marquee was switched to the girls' side in 1929 and is shown here on Whit Monday, 1936. Along with an orchestra which played on the terrace, the marquee was discontinued after 1939, although scaled-down reunions continued during the war.

Although the Old Crossleyans obviously had to suspend play, school matches continued during the Second World War, the 1943/4 team playing nineteen fixtures. From left to right, back row: G. Cash, G.D. Spencer, H. Wolstenholme, D. Gunton, J.T. Wadsworth, G. Matthews, J. Wardell, G. Britteon. Front row: J.G. Harrison, G. Sykes, C.J. Hughes, J. Ingham (captain), J.S. Pickles, C. Bates, G.H. Wood. Jack Ingham also captained the cricket team and represented the school at fives, joining the committee of the Old Scholars' Association in the 1950s and serving to this day, including six years as chairman.

From its inception there in 1900, the Old Boys' Association held meetings at the Boar's Head Hotel, soon switching to the school's reception room. In 1946, the former Vikings dormitory was converted into a war memorial room (pictured), using funds raised by the Old Scholars' Association. All Association meetings were held there and the room was available for social use four nights a week. In 1959, the Association transferred to the former laundry room behind the school and the vacated room became a physics laboratory in 1961. The cabinet beyond the snooker table, now located in the learning resource centre, still contains archive material dating back to the 1860s.

With the suspension of boarding in 1939, extensive dormitory and staff bedroom space became available on the upper two floors. The former Paladins dormitory was partitioned, creating a corridor and two spacious classrooms, P and Q. This is room Q in the late 1940s, showing the fifth form with Mr Raymond Clegg, senior French master. He taught at the school from 1943 to 1961, organising several trips to the Continent in the 1950s, and was actively involved in the highly successful dramatic society.

Between the wars, annual sports were held around Whitsuntide at Broomfield. During the 1940s, the annual sports moved to Thrum Hall and, in July 1946, the boys of Crossley and Porter, Heath and Sowerby Bridge participated in the first inter-grammar sports, held that year at the Shay Stadium. In 1948, boys' and girls' events were held together for the first time, with more schools competing. The boys, shown here with Mr Bolton and Mr Jack Kitching, took the junior, intermediate and overall shields that year. From 1952, both the school and the inter-grammar sports moved to Spring Hall.

In 1950, both the school (house) and inter-grammar sports were held at the Shay, on 8 and 15 June, respectively. Crossley and Porter girls' team made a clean sweep of the latter competition, taking the junior, intermediate, senior and overall shields and repeating the feat the following year. Later, Crossley and Porter girls were to take the overall championship every year from 1958 to 1968.

Although the girls held annual inter-house drama competitions between the wars, a boys' competition started only in autumn 1953. However, for a decade from 1948, in what was perhaps the golden age of Crossley and Porter costume drama, the schools' joint dramatic society put on a five-night performance each year in late winter. Jane Austen's *Pride and Prejudice* was chosen for 1950, filling the Halifax Playhouse from 7 to 11 February. The cast of twenty-two, the largest yet, included Wilfred Pickles' niece, Christine Pickles (far right), who would later pursue a television acting career in America, playing Judy Geller in *Friends*. From left to right: K. Jagger, Pat Walker, T.R. Sutcliffe, Margaret Foster, Margaret Akroyd, G. Kitson, J. Nicholl, June Normington, Maureen Timewell, Eileen Barker, S. O'Brien, Christine Pickles.

The staff of both the boys' and girls' schools, photographed together in 1954, with Miss Lightwood (headmistress, 1951-1955) and Mr Bolton (headmaster, 1941-1966) front row centre. On Mr Bolton's left is Mr John Lucas, who produced those splendid dramatic society plays, for which Mr Tom Gallagher (third, back row) and Miss Christine Walker (extreme right, front row) supervised construction of the set by the arts and handicrafts departments. Extreme left, front row, is Mr Clifford Hanson, who was about to retire after thirty-four years teaching French and English at the school.

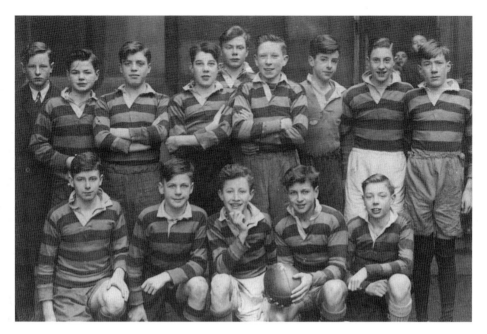

In autumn 1947, an under-fifteen team entered the Halifax and District Rugby League Championship and met with instant success, winning all nine games played. For several seasons thereafter, a Crossley and Porter under-fifteen team held sway on the local Rugby League scene, although teams from other Yorkshire towns tended to prove harder to beat. From left to right, back row: L. Greenwood, C. Forster, D. Brook, B. Ogden, R. Connew, H. Jenkins, P. Appleyard, G. Kitson, P. Leech. Front row: J.M. Sutcliffe, J. Crossley, T. Lewis, D. Elliott, J.K. Reynolds.

Among some excellent early 1950s school rugby teams, this 1952/3 First XV won fourteen of seventeen matches played. From left to right, back row: Roger Booth, Max Uttley, John Rodger, Bill Mount, Jack Shaw, Donald Whiteley, Geoffrey Whitaker, Roy Milliken, Christopher Wilkinson, Donald Short (P.E. teacher). Front row: Geoffrey Bryant, Trevor Lumb, Linford Tatham, Brian Randall (captain), Philip Webb, Roderick McKenzie, Jack Scroby. Tatham and McKenzie would later play for Halifax RUFC and represent Yorkshire. Scroby joined Bradford Northern in 1955, being transferred to Halifax for a then record fee of £7,500 in 1959 and later winning the championship.

In late 1954, a new dining room was created in the area which had once been the boys' large schoolroom. Beyond the serving hatches a new kitchen area was created from the original boys' form V room. Each table seated eight. At the boys' sitting the table head, usually a sixth former, served out the food which was brought from the hatches in tureens on trays by hapless 'fags', usually first form 'Bills'.

From 1921, the girls were taught cookery at Haugh Shaw and a domestic science course was introduced from September 1936, using Halifax Technical College twice a week. Toward the end of the Second World War, several former female staff bedrooms were converted into a self-contained flat which consisted of a sitting room, kitchen, bathroom and two bedrooms. Finally, in early 1951, the domestic science department was extended by conversion of part of the former Zoo dormitory and adjacent rooms, the largest of which is shown in 1954. Teaching was transferred to the extended technology block in 2005. From left to right: Sheila Blake, Dorothy Howe, Mary Helliwell, June Sladdin, Valerie Brooks, Betty Horsfall, Jean Sansom, Ann Wilby, Anne Whitaker.

After winning the Yorkshire Shield in 1956 and 1958, the Old Crossleyans savoured their greatest triumph in 1960 when they won 'T'Owd Tin Pot', the Yorkshire Cup, beating Sandal 9-0 in the final, played at Morley. From left to right, back row: S.S. Sparkes, F.N. Henderson, R.V. Aspinall, R.D.B. Thorpe, G. North, A.W. Whitham, C.R. Booth, D. McMahon, G. Whitaker, H. Wolstenholme, C.D. Ibbetson. Front row: D.G. Addenbrook, T. Driver, W.E. Hastings, J. Andrew, J.S. Bolton (president), C. Whitehouse, M. Uttley, G. Clayton, D.J. Barrett. Harry Wolstenholme later became the first player to complete 500 appearances for the Old Crossleyans.

The school's 1961/2 First XV won twenty of its twenty-five fixtures. From left to right, back row: Hinchliffe, ★Sunderland, Taylor, Weatherhead, Jackson, ★Healey, Barron, Smith, ★Ruddlesden. Front row: Collinge, Kennedy, ★Wilkinson, Gall (captain), ★Denton, ★Robinson, Squire. Paul Jackson, a teacher at the school in 2006, top-scored with 113 of the team's 385 points and went on to represent Yorkshire. In sevens (players marked ★ plus Whitaker), under the captaincy of Denton, the team met with considerable success, winning in Manchester and losing the Llanelli final only in extra time. With two changes, Wilkinson led another successful seven in 1963.

The annual reports indicate that netball was being played by 1921. An asphalt netball court was certainly in place by 1928. This doubled as a third tennis court in summer. In the 1959/60 season, the girls' senior netball team lost only once. From left to right, standing: Christine Wood, Wendy St Ruth, Susan Booth. Seated: Brenda Hornsey, Janet Wilkinson, Jean Naylor, Pamela Mitchell.

A music society was formed in December 1951, one objective being to encourage the performance of various instruments. Concerts featuring soloists or small groups of musicians were a regular feature of the next decade. In 1963, a school orchestra was formed, and by the summer of 1965 there were twenty-seven members, their instruments comprising twelve violins, three violas, two cellos, four clarinets, one oboe, two flutes, two trumpets and a piano. The orchestra is shown here *c.* 1964.

The centenary dinner, held on Friday 3 July 1964, was graced by several heads, past and present. From left to right: Miss E.M. Richardson, Miss L.E. Goodman, Mr J.S. Bolton, Mrs Bolton, Miss J. Lightwood. Miss Richardson, headmistress 1930-1951, had retired to her beloved Patterdale but continued to see many former pupils and kept in touch through *The Crossleyan*. Her successor, Miss Joan Lightwood, a graduate of Girton College, Cambridge, was principal of Epworth High School in Pietermaritzburg, South Africa from 1945 to 1950. While headmistress of the Crossley and Porter Girls' School from 1951, she respected and maintained the school's traditions and friendly atmosphere, while instituting the school council. She left to become head of the much larger Northampton Girls' Grammar School in 1955 and was succeeded by Miss Evelyn Goodman. Described as a 'considerable mathematician' with a 'formidable presence', Miss Goodman stressed the importance of rewarding students for making the fullest use of their academic ability and greatly valued the merit badge system, also keeping a keen eye on discipline and time-keeping. Forced to retire two years early through ill health in 1967, her popularity merited no fewer than six presentations, from students and staff to parents and old scholars, during her last week. Equally fondly remembered by generations of schoolboys, Mr Bolton, another mathematician, was headmaster from 1941 until his retirement in 1966. Keeping alive the Crossley spirit nurtured by his predecessor Mr Newport, he saw the school through the difficulties of the Second World War and the subsequent period of extensive structural improvements under the LEA. With a natural air of authority, 'Egg' Bolton nevertheless engendered a congenial atmosphere in the school, while earning the respect of staff and boys alike. His retirement brought to an end a period of ninety-four years under just three headmasters – truly the end of an era.

The school's centenary celebrations were held from Friday 3 July to Wednesday 8 July 1964. They included a procession of the whole school from the town hall to Square Church for a service of thanksgiving and rededication. A formal dinner (see opposite) was held in the school, attended by heads, staff and many former Crossleyans. On the Saturday, a buffet lunch was provided for old scholars, followed by the centenary bazaar. This aimed to raise a substantial sum to help establish a new school in Kilungu, Kenya. On the Monday, extensions to the playing fields and the new pavilion at Standeven House were formally opened. A gymnastic display (pictured) at Broomfield involved the whole school and included a demonstration of physical training as given in Victorian and Edwardian times. Mr John Vaughan (art master), resplendent in whiskers, top hat and frock coat, playing the formidable Mr Barber, commanded the army of pupils. Also performed were maypole, aesthetic, country and modern dancing and club swinging. On the Tuesday and Wednesday, the school was open to parents and the general public, who enjoyed a varied programme of lessons, films, music, drama and demonstrations, thus giving them an opportunity to share in the school's life in the centenary year.

The boys' school staff, shortly before Mr Bolton's retirement in summer 1966. Standing, left to right: Messrs A. Atkinson, T. Ryan, D. Ainley, R.A. Davies, T. Walls, J. Vaughan, J. Gott, J. Tennant, R. Knott, K. Ludlam. Seated: Messrs M. Uttley, G. Knott, J.L. Davies, J.W. Lucas, J.S. Bolton (headmaster), J. Brearley, T. Gallagher, C.W. Thorp, P.J. Rushworth. Mr John W. Lucas, on the staff since 1947, became acting head until the merger with the girls' school on 1 January 1968, after which he was headmaster until his death in September 1970.

One of the last staff photographs before the amalgamation of the girls' and boys' schools shows headmistress Miss Evelyn Goodman (front row, centre), just before her retirement in 1967. Miss Jean Thomson, her deputy, is on her right. One feature of the period was the growing number of men who were appointed to the girls' school, a presage of the amalgamation soon to come.

In 1952, a start was made on construction of modern laboratories on the south-west (girls') side of the school. By 1962, there were two top-floor laboratories for each of the sciences: biology, chemistry and physics. Miss Houghton is shown *c.* 1964 supervising microscopy in the girls' biology laboratory, designated C14 in 2006. The boys' laboratory was next door to the right, where Mr Gott taught at the time.

Annual speech days were suspended during the Second World War, restarting in December 1947 as separate events for the boys' and girls' schools. A single annual event was reintroduced after unification of the two schools from 1 January 1968. This group of prize winners, shown in the following academic year 1968/9, includes the head boy, John Swallow, and head girl, Lesley Priestley, seated centre.

Looking westward along Free School Lane (right), this aerial view of the school is thought to date from the mid-1960s, when the boys' (B) and girls' (G) schools were still technically separate. (1) The two lawn tennis courts, devoid of nets and quite worn, suggesting this is an early autumn view. (2) The cenotaph, erected in 1920 and rededicated in 1949. (3) The cricket nets, work on which was started by the boys themselves in 1910, under the supervision of the recently arrived headmaster, Mr Newport. (4) The athletics arena, clearly showing the two semi-circular high jump areas. The long jump and pole vault runway is hidden by the line of trees. The triple jump runway is adjacent to the new wing and fives courts. The arena was laid out after the Second World War. (5) Boys' gymnasium. The small extension toward the main building was built in 1921 as the first boys' changing room, later becoming the PE master's equipment room. (6) Boys' new wing, opened in 1930. (7) Fives courts, opened 1928. (8) The workshop, modernised and extended in the 1950s to include a drawing office and metalwork shop (beneath skylight). In 2006, this building is linked to the new technology block built on the site of the fives courts. (9) Boys' playground, the top pitch. Note the two tennis courts, installed around 1950. (10) The back (north) lodge. The school bought a minibus in 1977 and some work was carried out to convert the lodge into a garage. It was never completed. The front (south) lodge is out of view to the left. (11) Girls' playground. There had been four tennis courts in 1950. (12) Girls' new wing, opened in 1930 and extended in 2005 to form the language block.

In 1968, the boys' and girls' houses were merged, creating four new houses: Crossley (Trojans and St David's), Porter (Vikings and St Patrick's), Savile (Spartans and St Andrew's) and Standeven (Paladins and St George's). This large 1968/9 group of prefects includes house captains in the front row, from left to right: Patricia Roberts (Porter), Martyn Bradshaw (Savile), Joan Sleight (Crossley), Stefan Sotnyk (Standeven), Pearl Ainsley (deputy head girl), John Swallow (head boy), Lesley Priestley (head girl), Peter Sloane (deputy head boy), Jean Graham (Standeven), Chad Fowler (Crossley), Kathryn Jagger (Savile), David Wadsworth (Porter).

Mr Brian Evans, shown here with a group of prefects in 1973, was appointed to succeed Mr Lucas as headmaster in January 1971. He came from Duffryn High School, Newport, prior to which he had been head of history at Heath. His period of six years in charge reflected wider changes in secondary education at the time. Among new subjects introduced by him were environmental studies and economics. In 1977, he left to become head of Honley High School.

Above: A fourth form group, with Mr P. Williams, in September 1976. Fourth from right, back row, is Brian Moore. He attended Crossley and Porter School from 1973 to 1980, captaining the school rugby team in every year apart from his first. While captaining the First XV in 1979/80, he also played for the Old Crossleyans. Ironically, earlier in his school career, Brian had played in a variety of positions in the backs, before eventually excelling as hooker.

Below: After leaving the school, Brian studied law at Nottingham University, passed the Law Society's final examinations and was articled to a solicitor's practice in Nottingham. Meanwhile, his rugby career

continued to flourish, first with Roundhay and then with Nottingham. He was selected for the England under-twenty-three tour to Spain and then toured Italy with England B in 1985. In April 1987, Brian was picked for England's Calcutta Cup match against Scotland and then played in three World Cup matches, becoming a regular fixture in the team the following season. While playing club rugby for Harlequins, he was a member of England's Grand Slam winning team in 1991, having also toured Australia with the British Lions. Brian went on to break the record for England caps for a hooker. Well known for his robust play, he would never take a backward step. The law is his profession but his voice and no-nonsense opinions are familiar from his television commentaries.

In 1981, the junior string quartet won their section of the National Chamber Music Competition for Schools, beating sixty-five other quartets, including some from specialist music schools. From left to right: Jonathan Moulds (viola), Christopher Moulds (cello), Julia Hanson (violin), Gary Best (violin), the leader. Both Jonathan and Gary were sixteen at the time of the 1982 competition, forcing the quartet into the senior section, where, much to their credit, they reached the national final.

The 1981 staff with, centre front row, Mr Paul Barker, headmaster from 1977 to 1991. Either side of him are his deputies, Mr R.B. Atkinson and Mrs P. Barker on his right and Mr P.F. Fowler on his left. Seated, second left, Mr Philip Webb, a former pupil, spent his entire teaching career at the school between 1958 and 1999. In 1985, the amalgamation with Heath would temporarily swell staff and pupil numbers to 70 and 1,100 respectively.

School Heads 1864-1985

1864	Mr Bithell
1864-1872	Mr Arthur Oliver
1872-1910	Mr William Cambridge Barber
1910-1941	Mr George Bernard Newport
1941-1966	Mr John Stanley Bolton
1968-1970	Mr John Whitaker Lucas
1971-1977	Mr Brian Evans
1977-1985	Mr Paul Barker

Girls' School Headmistresses 1877-1967

1877-1879	Miss Bowen
1879-1880	Miss Larritt
1880-1892	Miss Angela Louisa Collins
1892-1897	Miss Wayte
1897-1913	Miss Dora Knight
1913-1929	Miss Mary Elizabeth Dale
1930-1951	Miss Richardson
1951-1955	Miss Joan Lightwood
1955-1967	Miss Evelyn Goodman

five

Crossley
Heath School
1985-2006

The merger of Heath with Crossley and Porter to form Crossley Heath School took place in 1985, after 400 years and 121 years respectively. The first head was Mr Paul Barker, previous head of Crossley and Porter School, who led a school of about 1,100 students which used the two sites until 1988. This reduced to around 700 by 1990 before increasing to around 1,000 currently. The late 1980s saw a period of continuous debate about the future direction of the new school amongst all interested parties – parents, governors and Calderdale Council. There was uncertainty over moves towards comprehensive education, further amalgamations and the creation of sixth form teaching centres. Academic success continued to flourish after amalgamation – perhaps the friendly rivalry encouraged healthy competition!

The 1988 Education Reform Act enabled the creation of grant-maintained schools, free of council control and directly funded by the government. Mr Barker retired after fourteen years in 1991 at the stage when Crossley Heath became grant-maintained, one of the first schools in Calderdale to do so. Mr John Bunch, former head at Heath, succeeded Mr Barker, taking the school through this opt-out phase. Year-on-year results continued to improve despite the enormous pace of change in education, with such innovations as AS levels (as part of the Curriculum 2000 changes) putting pressure on both staff and students. In September 1998 Crossley Heath was one of only seventy-five schools awarded the status of Beacon School, a government initiative encouraging the sharing of good practice by working in partnership with other schools, and developing new ideas across all areas of the curriculum. Funding for the Beacon scheme finished in 2003. By 1999 arrangements for self-funding schools meant that they became known as Foundation Schools. Changes included funding once again coming from Calderdale, and the governing body undergoing constitutional change.

Mr Bunch retired in 2001 and Miss Helen Gaunt was appointed as head, vowing to continue to balance tradition with new ideas and strategies. One of the most important successes of her leadership has been the achievement of Language College status in 2003, allowing further refurbishment of that wing of the school. Extra languages offered include Spanish, Italian, Chinese and Urdu. An International Day has become an annual event and results have continued to improve steadily, so that Crossley Heath School is now among the highest performing state schools in the country.

Despite the grade two-listed building being described unkindly in the 1993 OFSTED report as 'old and rambling', it has undergone massive renovation and during the 1990s major work was completed on refurbishing the roof and all main areas of the school By July 2005 the technology block was extended and now houses all technologies. This concludes work that really began in 2001 when the redundant fives courts were demolished to provide technology accommodation. Music and debating continue to thrive in school as does the annual creation of Young Enterprise 'companies'. Additionally, in 2005 the Artsmark Award was presented for good practice in arts provision. Ambitious plans were put forward to build a state-of-the-art sports hall in 1997 but unfortunately funding could not be found to allow it to go ahead. Acquiring modern sports facilities remains high on the agenda today and in spite of obvious limitations, the school has been awarded the Sportsmark by the Sports Council for commitment to physical education and sports provision. Sporting achievements feature in every annual report and not just for the sports taught in school. Students achieve locally, nationally and internationally. A recent highlight was the school First XV rugby team winning the *Daily Mail* Vase at Twickenham in March 2005.

Above left: Mr John Bunch.

Above right: A close look at the Crossley Heath School badge reveals a traditional style that amalgamates the origins of both Heath and Crossley and Porter Schools. The abbreviated Latin motto of Heath, which translated means 'The seal of the free grammar school of Queen Elizabeth in the vicarage of Halifax', surrounds the Tudor symbols of a rose and portcullis, and the open book shows the first line of Lily's *Latin Grammar*. The scroll retains the Crossley family and Crossley and Porter motto: *Omne bonum ab alto,* meaning 'All good things come from above'. The animal is a demi-hind and is holding a crosslet, or small cross. An art teacher, Mr Jeremy Burgoyne, designed the new badge.

Above left: Close inspection of the Crossley Heath clock tower reveals it to be a work of art in itself. However, after well over 100 years the tower deteriorated to a point where the clock had stopped and drastic building repairs were required. Grants, together with fund-raising led by Jackson Brown, Nicola Dodgson and Dawn Wilcock of the sixth form, enabled all the renovation work to be completed in the early 1990s. Complicated scaffolding was required to reach the decorative lead work on the tower. Wooden moulds were made for the four horseshoe shapes, with the lead then moulded around the outside. The clock itself is very unusual, the design dating back over 300 years. It is a flat bed clock made by Joyce of Whitchurch in 1846, even though the school was not completed until 1864, and is one of a few examples which is still hand-wound. The three weights from the clock, each weighing 350kg, are wound by hand up from the cellar and will keep accurate time for about a week. One of the three bells which chimes on the quarter hour is a massive bronze hour bell, described by an expert as 'the Rolls Royce' of bells. The half-hour bell was often used as a funeral bell and on the occasion of the death of King George VI in 1952 it was rung fifty-six times. Tradition determines that being a clock winder is a position held by sixth formers, the names of whom are recorded in the tower, the earliest being J. Rutherford in 1889.

Above right: Nicola Dodgson and Jackson Brown make the final inspection of the renovated clock tower.

Opposite below: Upper Sixth students on a trip to the French town of Boulogne in 1993, as part of their French A-Level studies, being immersed in French culture and practising language skills. They travelled by school minibus with Mr John Morton, and all luggage was on the roof! Annual trips abroad from Crossley and Porter School had begun by the early fifties and are still a regular feature of school life today.

Above: In this picture, of September 1991, students of all ages in house teams are involved in Sci-Tech 91, a competition to design a vehicle powered by a falling mass attached to the vehicle, which was timed as it travelled along a six-metre track. The relatively new Crossley Heath uniform is easy to see here with its black blazer, white shirt, black tie with gold stripe, and silver tie with gold and black stripes for sixth form. Allowing girls to wear trousers was still about ten years away and by 2004 all sixth form uniform was made optional.

Staff in 1994 looking much less formal than in days gone by, all part of a team of teachers and support staff running a modern school. The headmaster is John Bunch with deputy heads Tony Rickwood and Honoree Gordon shown too. It is symbolic of the continuity of staff and their enjoyment of teaching at the school that so many retired from Crossley Heath after between twenty-five and forty years' service in the school in its various incarnations.

Students in 1996 trying their hand at journalism, producing the school newspaper of the time, *The Crossley Heath Chronicle*, supervised by Mrs Sally Bunch, the main editor. Producing school journals has always been popular, the first issue being in 1883. From left to right, back row: Joshua Fielden, Eleanor Taylor, Emily Sheard, Ben Helliwell. Front row: Vicky Walsh, Alexa George, Katharine James, Julia Brooke, Nikola Butler.

Rugby squad from 1998/9 with coach and former Heath student Mr Steve Donlan. From left to right, back row: Liam Kennedy, Chris Wade, Peter Clegg, Will Jordan, Michael Knowles, David Hindle. Middle row: Jonathan McDonnell, Chris Greenwood, Stuart Hill, Martin Brook, Gary Bolton, Martin Wood, Robert Siswick. Front row: Alex Stott, Chris Irving, Mansoor Riaz, Aaron Camplin, Alastair Fielding, Jonathan Wade, James Wainwright. Irving also played for the England A under sixteen team.

Skiing holidays began in 1963 with twenty-two students spending Christmas in Kanderstag, Switzerland. This 1998 group is representative of holidays taken in Montafon, Austria, in the same valley for over twenty years, mainly because of the quality and variety of skiing and the friendships built up with the locals and the ski instructors: 'Ah, the Englisher gruppa'. Skiing is in four different areas locally, providing something suitable for everyone – roll on February half-term!

Above: March 1998 saw the first mixed cast of both staff and students in the presentation of the musical *Oliver*, directed by Mr Gordon Stansfield. The audience will always remember him as Mr Bumble, with

Mr Dave Cheesmond as Bill Sykes, Mr Paul Dignum as Mr Sowerberry, Mr Andrew Coote as Dr Grimwig and, as shown, Mr Philip Webb as Fagin, with Matthew Duddridge as the Artful Dodger and Robert Quinn as Oliver Twist.

Left: On the steps to success are top-grade A-Level students in 1999, helping to put Crossley Heath among the top schools in the North of England and continuing the trend of significant academic improvement since becoming grant-maintained in 1991. A-Level, GCSE and Key Stage 3 SATS results were at a record high. Curriculum changes at this time included the introduction of sports studies despite the shortcomings of the facilities. From left to right, back row: Matthew Wright, Joanne Bintliff, Rebecca Griffiths, Jenny Teal, Ross Jones. Middle row: Rachel Thompson, Madiha Hasan, Rebecca Thorley. Front row: Andrew Fowler, -?-.

C.P.S.
Hx

Dear Val

Thanks very much for your note. I didn't quite know whether the first one was from you or not – Harrison giggled so much when he gave it to me, that I thought it was a fudge note from him. I compared the writing with that on the Xmas card you sent me. By the way! Thanks very much for it. I was rather mad when I received it because Mother is so fearfully against me having letters from boys. – so for Heaven's sake don't write to me in the holidays.

I'm glad you weren't reported the other night. We were all wondering if Mr. Harrison would go to Lizzie. It's a good thing he didn't or else there would have been a row.

Yours,
E.M.

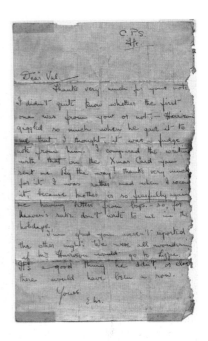

Far left: Agnes Enid Mitchell (Enid). She was born on 2 May 1907 and admitted to the orphanage in January 1917.

Left: Arthur Carley Varley (Val). He was born on 2 May 1908 and admitted to the orphanage in September 1916.

During renovation work in 2000 a bundle of twenty-three letters, dating from 1917/8 from Enid to 'Val', was found beneath some floorboards hidden on the rafters of the room below, formerly the boys' boot room in the cellar, where they changed from outdoor to indoor footwear. The correspondence, which had survived the passage of time fairly intact, was seemingly between two girls, although it turned out that Val was Arthur Carley Varley. The letters were sent using go-betweens (other named orphans), and delivery probably took place in the pantry, a room off the dining room where all the orphans ate together. Mention is made of 'choice week' about which nothing is known, playing 'truths' and of who likes whom. While boys and girls were not completely segregated, any such correspondence or relationship would have been strictly forbidden.

Arthur went to work at a gentlemen's outfitters in Halifax after he left the orphanage while Enid went on to teach in London before going on to get a first in the history of education at Bangor University.

Harlech, June 2000 – playing rounders with a tent peg! The highlight of year eight, if not the whole of their school time, was the five-day camping trip to Harlech on the Welsh coast, organised for many years by the late Mr Richard Fleming. A hectic schedule included horse riding, ecology and walks up Snowdon, visits to a slate mine and Harlech Castle, and beach activities on the extensive sands. With sixth formers acting as supervisors and teachers acting as master chefs, together with the insomniac activities of students, abiding memories were provided for all concerned with the annual Harlech trip!

New mode of school transport in Cairo for some of the students lucky enough to go on the millennium cruise in 2000. Onshore visits took in Israel, Jerusalem and Bethlehem, the ancient Turkish city of Ephesus, Istanbul, Cairo and the pyramids, Tutankhamen and the Dead Sea – all helping students to put the last 2,000 years in context.

Right: Girls' football began *c.* 1998 and is now an established school sport right from year seven, with teams playing in the Calderdale and West Yorkshire leagues. Coached by Miss Amy Taylor, this 2000 team are, from left to right, back row: Stephanie Berry, Sophie Pickersgill, Nicola Shaw, Claire McCamley. Front row: Natalie Thorn, Cassie Barker, Sam Morris.

Below: Wearing a tuxedo or ballgown and going to the ball is now an established part of leaving school and, from 2004, year thirteen have also had a photographic yearbook produced as a memento of their time at Crossley Heath. In May 2001 the girls are looking gorgeous! From left to right: Kirsty Lindsay, Rebecca Letven, Philippa Snellgrove, Emily Jackson, Rachel Taylor, Kylie Hall, Anna Jones, Annette Berry, Louisa O'Connor, Natalie Spencer.

After studying Tennessee Williams' *A Streetcar named Desire* as part of their A-Level English literature course, the Crossley Heath School Charity Committee and others decided they could raise money at the same time by staging the play in April 2001. £670 was donated to Cancer Research UK. From left to right: Filipo Nenna as Harold Mitchell, Matthew Schofield as Stanley Kowalski, Greg Collingridge as Pablo Gonzales and Oliver Gilford as Steve Hubbel.

Rugby Union has a long and honourable tradition that goes back into the history of all three schools. Crossley Heath School has taken successful rugby tours to Ireland and the Isle of Man for many years and, building on those foundations, tours further afield began in 2000 to Canada and in 2004 to Australia. Here the school touring team, led by Mr Neil Hale and captained by Richard Carling, are seen after their victory over Linpark High School from Pietermaritzburg, during their South Africa tour in summer 2002.

Right: The Parents' Association (PTA), formed in 1945 and now called the Crossley Heath Association (CHA), has always existed to support the school through building and maintaining a partnership between parents, teachers and others associated with the school. Everyone will recall their own Christmas parties and some will be amazed to note that the tradition of country dancing still continues! Lesley Wood, previous chair, together with treasurer Chris Wainwright, is seen presenting £15,000 to Miss Helen Gaunt, head teacher, in 2002, at the start of fund-raising for language college status.

Above left: People's Park, Halifax, was one of the many benefactions associated with the Crossley family. Francis Crossley's house, Belle Vue, overlooked a twelve-acre site which he developed in August 1857 after a visit to New England. In 1860, a large statue of Francis Crossley was erected with the present bandstand added in 1879. The park fell into decline over the years until a restoration programme between 1995 and 2002 transformed the park to its former glory, with a formal reopening on Friday 20 September 2002 by Lord Somerleyton, the great grandson of Sir Francis Crossley. On that occasion, the Crossley Heath Wind Band was proud to entertain guests from the beautifully restored bandstand.

Above right: Lord and Lady Somerleyton.

Left: Mrs Joan Tidswell, chair of the governors of Crossley Heath School until 2005, seen here in summer 2003 celebrating twenty-five years in that post. She has been a governor since 1971 in her capacity as a local councillor and hence has played a leading role in the lives of both Crossley and Porter and Crossley Heath Schools. Joan (*née* Spurr) was a day girl at the school from 1936 to 1942 and became an active member of the Old Crossleyans' Association. She later married Gordon, also a former Crossleyan.

Below: Representing students across the school houses, the range of sports and all age groups, the annual sports presentation evening, organised by Ms Liz Oldfield, is a recently established date on the school calendar. Seen here at the usual venue, Standeven House, in July 2003 are, from left to right: Georgina Denham, Edwin Prior, Katie Foster, Kevin McCallion (coach at Halifax RUFC and former Crossley and Porter student), Kyle Wild, Rachel Taylor, Ben Craddock.

Several thousand pounds are raised for charity every year with an enormous variety of events managed by a committee led by sixth formers and a teacher. Miss Claire Bradberry, a former Crossley Heath student, is seen here in July 2003 with some of the students who raised £9,000 that year. Popular events include non-uniform days, talent shows, especially those featuring singing and dancing staff groups, and a sponge-the-teacher session.

Top A-Level grades for the girls in 2003 helped to give the school almost sixty per cent grades A and B at A-Level. From left to right: Ellen Davies, Pippa Marson, Kate Walton, Rachael France, Sarah Jones and Claire Ward.

Celebrating being awarded specialist Language College status from September 2003 are, from left to right: Sloane Mills, Elizabeth Uttley, Matthew Wilson, Katie Lake. The school was required to raise £50,000, which it did with sponsorship help from the Crossley Heath Association and both former schools' Old Scholars' Associations amongst others. The Language Wing has been extended creating two extra classrooms with improved facilities include an ICT suite and the latest in learning technology and resources, and is also open outside of school hours.

A fairly recent addition to the Crossley Heath calendar has been Higher Education Week, held in July each year. Year twelve students become familiarised with the stages involved in progressing into higher education. Links have been established with academic institutions and several universities help students with the processes involved in the next step of their careers after leaving school. From left to right, school officials for 2003/4 are: Kerrell Cronly, Juwairia Akram, Dr Roger Ash (Bradford University), Ian Taylor, Barnabas Calvert.

The twenty-nine students plus staff who visited China in October 2003 returned with memories of such spectacular sights as the Great Wall of China, Tian'anmen Square, the Forbidden City, the Terracotta Army and Beijing. This trip, together with a study visit to China by head teacher Helen Gaunt, proved to be a good forerunner to subsequent links with schools in China and a return visit by twelve Chinese teachers. In addition to offering Mandarin Chinese language, Crossley Heath also now hosts a Chinese student teacher at school each year.

A group of year thirteen students in September 2003 at the edge of the River Avon at Averton Gifford, studying vegetation of a salt marsh. Mr Steve Eggleton has led biology trips to Slapton Ley Field Centre, a nature reserve in South Devon, for many years. The Ley is the largest natural freshwater lake in the West Country and as it is just inland from the sea, students experience working in freshwater, marine and terrestrial habitats. Badger watching at night is an annual highlight.

Above: The annual prize-giving awards ceremony in the autumn term recognises achievement in academic, sporting and other areas, with Halifax Parish Church as the current venue. Guests enjoy listening to a high-profile speaker together with music provided by the school orchestra and choirs. In 2003, from left to right, back row: Saqib Bashir, Aparna Mathur, Richard Armitage, Lydia Fox. Front row: Tracey Mollet, Miss Helen Gaunt (head teacher), Danny Garside.

Left: Students always return from the annual battlefields trip with a greater sense of compassion for those affected by events of the First World War, particularly having visited the memorial to Captain Mander, a former teacher at Crossley and Porter Orphan Home and School (see p.71). The 2004 tour, led by Mr Steve Donlan, head of history, visited Ypres Salient, Belgium and the Somme region of France. Shown at the Menin Gate memorial are, from left to right: Jeffrey Mak, Mr Paul Jackson and Isobel Chillman. Both Mr Donlan and Mr Jackson attended Heath Grammar School.

The languages department trip to the Rhineland in May 2004 was characterised by sun and fun as students visited Koblenz, Ruddesheim, Boppard and Bonn. Other language trip destinations include Normandy and an exchange visit to Aachen, twin town to Halifax. In 2006 there is a trip planned to Murcia in Spain. The picture shows Laura Thackray and Katie Griffiths outside a café in Bonn.

Netball continues to be the major girls' sport at Crossley Heath, with participation in tournaments in all years and entry into the Calderdale league system from year eight. This under-eighteen team was particularly successful as one of the top teams in Calderdale, and also enjoyed coaching younger players. From left to right, back row: Aimee Driver, Katey Steven, Claire Smith. Front row: Rachel Turner, Roz Cox, Emma Penny, Emma Kershaw, Claire Taylforth.

House drama is a popular annual event which gives everyone the opportunity to contribute, whether through acting or behind the scenes. Queen's House was on a winning streak in 2004, having triumphed again with their production of *Aladdin*. From left to right: Hannah Tryl as Princess Jasmine, Luke Tryl as Jafar, Robert Young as the sultan, Gareth Hunter as Jasmine's pet tiger, Raja and Andrew Young as Iago the parrot.

Plays are chosen, produced and directed entirely by the students, with no staff help at all – something of a test of fortitude and character on the part of house captains. Porter House came second with their production of *Dracula* in 2004. From left to right: Sam Dumigan, Connor Michael, James Sykes, James Rainford, Verity Hyland, Alex Burnett, Helen Wright.

Limited time available demands that each play be relatively short, perhaps forty-five minutes or so to allow all four productions to be shown in one day. Savile House produced *Beauty and the Beast* in 2004. The house system continues to be strongly upheld, with the names King's and Queen's originating from Heath School, and Savile and Porter from Crossley and Porter School.

The production of *Robin Hood, Men in Tights* allowed King's House to carry on the Heath School tradition of boys wearing female attire in the school play! Heath was of course a boys' school. From left to right: Jonathan Marshall as Little John, Gawen Davies, Arshad Ali as Robin Hood, David Anderson as the guard, James Mallard, James Wise.

Above: Over the years hockey replaced lacrosse after difficulties were encountered finding opposing teams. However, lacrosse has seen a revival of late, being introduced in year eleven as a new sporting challenge, despite still using original Crossley and Porter equipment complete with inscribed names! Field hockey is a thing of the past, with the modern game entirely played on AstroTurf, meaning matches for Crossley Heath are 100 per cent away games. The under-fifteen team in 2004 are, from left to right, back row: Keeley Sherrard, Alice Holleworth, Francesca Parker, Stephanie Wood, Hester Lomas. Front row: Sarah Noble, Melanie Sutcliffe, Rebecca Bell, Amy Greenwood, Hannah Jeffrey.

Left: Students participated in Sport Relief in July 2004, a national event where 81,000 people ran 'the biggest mile event in history'. The 'Go the Extra Mile' campaign was adopted to mark the fiftieth anniversary of Sir Roger Bannister's four-minute mile, with the aim of raising millions of pounds to tackle worldwide poverty. Crossley Heath students, including this pair, Hollie Heffernan and Sophie Uttley, spent their lunchtime running round the moor with their customary enthusiasm for joining in charitable fun events.

Right: Celebrating one year as a language college on International Day, July 2004, an annual event now suspending normal lessons and involving the whole school in a range of activities. Besides taster sessions in many languages, other activities include dancing, music and sports, quizzes and understanding international trade. In 2005 Crossley Heath was awarded the Artsmark Award for showing commitment to the full range of arts and pictured creating Aboriginal art silk painting are, from left to right, back: Ms Alison Saldana, Mr Glyn Hirst, head of art. Front: Emma Beal, Francesca Turner, Katie Travis.

Below: The inter-house swimming gala is an annual event held at Halifax Swimming Pool, this one in 2004. Whilst Crossley Heath School can boast a swimming pool of its own, its size inhibits all but the smallest events! However, despite this, in 1911, the school managed a swimming gala where besides the usual swimming strokes, there was a race with lighted candles, blindfolds and 'writing in the water'. As a finale, Mrs Milner, the swimming instructress, gave an exhibition which included 'Swimming in walking attire', and 'Undressing on the surface of the water'!

The annual carol service has become part of the Crossley Heath tradition and is held at the Halifax Parish Church. With the increase in size of school population during the 1990s, it is currently the only venue where the entire school gathers together. With little room to spare, the service attracts former students and parents too. A full programme of musical events and readings every year means there is little time left to notice the nearby statue of Dr Favour, founder of Heath Grammar School, observing the changes to the scholarly congregation.

Chief inspector of schools, David Bell, visited in January 2005 and was impressed by the wide range of activities and interests going on in school despite the shortcomings of the building. He was struck by the enthusiasm of students and staff, commenting that he believed that existing grammar schools are here to stay. Students with offers from Oxford or Cambridge are, from left to right: Helen Newsome, Lisa Drury, Luke Tryl, Tracey Mollet, Ruth Rushworth, Nicola Cooper, Emma Mackrell, Kathryn McArdle.

The alternative non-uniform day in January 2005! Staff are doing their bit to raise funds for the Asian tsunami disaster by taking part in the most successful fund-raising appeal of the year. The picture includes head boy, Luke Tryl and head girl, Angela Crossley.

Pictured in Seville at Easter 2005, twenty-five students and four staff, led by language teacher Mr Ian Kendrick, took part in the first Crossley Heath trip to Spain, following the introduction of Spanish to the curriculum. From Malaga in southern Spain the group headed to Seville, on to Cordova and finally Granada. All agreed it was a very positive trip with lots of culture and history, together with a good measure of shopping and fun.

Left: Some of the sixty-eight students in the choir performing abroad for the very first time at Easter 2005. Led by the head of music, Mrs Pam Roberts, the choir, windband and string group travelled to Spain. They are seen here performing in the bandstand at Pablo D'Espagnol, Barcelona, conducted by music teacher Mrs Angela Stradling. Music within school has moved into the twenty-first century with computer technology existing alongside traditional instruments. Future plans involve international collaboration on musical projects, whilst house music continues to be a popular annual event.

Below: Geography field trip looking at features of glaciation in the Langdale Pikes, May 2005. Crossley Heath was chosen as 'Best selective state school for boys for geography at AS Level' by the *Good Schools Guide* in 2004, after the results from this year thirteen group. They are shown with their teachers who are, from left to right: Mr Roger Campbell, Mr Rod Kay (head of geography) and Mr John Fielding.

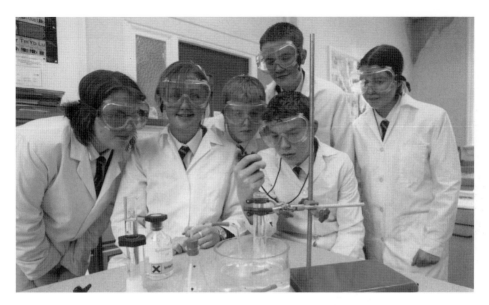

GCSE students (from left to right) Beth Harvey, Natalie Fern, Ben Beresford, Ryan Meadowcroft, Richard Wood and Sarah Noble are representative of 2005, the year that Crossley Heath achieved its best ever exam results at GCSE (99.4 per cent gaining 5 A★ to C grades) and A-Level, helping the school achieve its position as the top choice in Calderdale. Improving facilities for the expanding sixth form is a school priority, although being a grade two-listed building always complicates development plans.

The days of 'Silence Please' passed on when the old library was transformed into a modern learning resource centre opened by author Robert Swindells in 1995. A fancy dress competition for years seven and eight is the finale to the annual book week. Seen here in November 2005 are characters from many stories including a complement of witches, lions and a wardrobe! Medal-winning speakers over recent years have included Beverley Naidoo, Bali Rai, and Melvin Burgess.

Left: Sophie Cox is an international judo player and ranked seventh in the world in May 2005, competing in the under 57kg weight division. Sophie started playing judo when she was six and successfully managed to combine her sporting career with her education, attending Crossley Heath School from 1993 to 2000. She is a member of the National Judo Academy at Bisham Abbey National Sports Centre and is ranked first in Great Britain and second in Europe (December 2005). Sophie has won countless medals but her greatest achievements are her bronze medal from the Commonwealth Games in 2002 and representing Great Britain in the Athens Olympics in 2004.

Below: While the academic results for 2004/5 at A-Level and GCSE were the best ever recorded, this rugby success, winning the *Daily Mail* Vase at Twickenham in March 2005, represents much of the true spirit of Crossley Heath School. Through hard work, team spirit, commitment and a belief in themselves the squad rose to every challenge and succeeded. Everyone involved – the players, the staff and the parents – have fantastic memories which they will treasure for the rest of their lives.

Above: Official opening of the Tidswell Rooms (language block), July 2005. From left to right: Stephanie Berry (head girl), Blessing Essang, Mrs Joan Tidswell, Mr Gordon Tidswell, The Mayor, Cllr John C. Williamson, James Lawson (head boy), Chris Vine.

Right: Message from the Head Teacher, Miss Helen Gaunt.

The images in this book show that its success can be attributed primarily to the dedication, enthusiasm and contribution made by staff, students and governors. The staff over the years have always been this school's most valuable resource. Students are willing to help, eager to learn and actively involved in decision making. Their enthusiasm for the school and everything that goes on is infectious and cannot help but leave visitors feeling impressed.

I hope that you have enjoyed this book. I would like to thank all of those who have gone before me and those who are still to come for the privilege of being included in the historic recordings of this fine school!

Finally, and most importantly, I hope that the ethos engendered over the years will continue to develop long into the future.

Other local titles published by Tempus

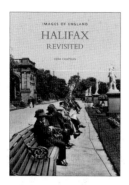

Halifax Revisited

VERA CHAPMAN

Halifax has an industrial past of woollen mills, canals and railways, the wharves and stations of which liberally dot the countryside. The town today reflects the changes wrought by the Victorians, who created broad streets and fine buildings. This collection of over 200 archive images illustrates the history of Halifax as it once was and records how the town has developed since the mid-eighteenth century.

7524 3047 5

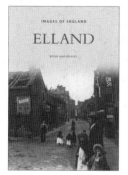

Elland

BRIAN HARGREAVES

This fascinating collection of over 180 archive photographs taken by Albert Townsend, a local photographer of the early twentieth century, captures the Elland of the last 150 years, including busy streets, churches, public houses and industry. This pictorial history, supported by accompanying text, takes in the transition of the town from Victorian tenements through the life and death of the textile industry to the arrival of the modern tramway, linking Elland to its larger neighbours.

7524 3703 8

Brighouse and District

CHRIS HELME

This fascinating collection of archive photographs illustrates some of the historical developments which have shaped the town of Brighouse. The Industrial Revolution brought new prosperity to the area, and this book describes the effects of industrialisation on the town and its people. Informative captions bring additional colour to the images, exploring the buildings, transport and shops of Brighouse and its surrounding settlements, as well as the close-knit communities which have formed the heart of the area.

7524 3577 9

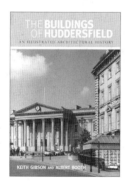

The Buildings of Huddersfield

KEITH GIBSON AND ALBERT BOOTH

Huddersfield has a surprisingly rich building heritage, and this fascinating volume explores the streets of the town, documenting and discussing the buildings and architectural features which may be missed in the everyday hustle and bustle of life. Keith Gibson and Albert Booth show how the changing demands of population, business and industry have shaped the town's architecture and with a splendid series of photographs illustrates their historical narrative to great effect.

7524 3675 9

If you are interested in purchasing other books published by Tempus, or in case you have difficulty finding any Tempus books in your local bookshop, you can also place orders directly through our website

www.tempus-publishing.com